Undoing Homophobia in Primary Schools

The *No Outsiders* Project Team

(compiled by Elizabeth Atkinson and Renée DePalma)

Trentham Books

Stoke on Trent, UK and Sterling, USA

Trentham Books Limited
Westview House   22883 Quicksilver Drive
734 London Road   Sterling
Oakhill   VA 20166-2012
Stoke on Trent   USA
Staffordshire
England ST4 5NP

First published 2010

British Library Cataloguing-in-Publication Data
A catalogue record for this book is available from the British
Library

ISBN 978 1 85856 440 1

Designed and typeset by Trentham Books Ltd and printed in
Great Britain by Cromwell Press Group, Trowbridge

Undoing Homophobia in Primary Schools

Contents

Foreword
Gillian Klein

Jenny lives on

Once upon a time, there was a little girl called Jenny. *Jenny lived with Eric and Martin.* And Jenny lives on…

I was asked to write the foreword to this book because I have a story to tell that the editors wanted to appear in it. It's flattering none the less to be part of, as well as publisher, of this important and inspiring book.

My story is not about Jenny but about the book in which she appears. Jenny is the name given to the little Danish girl Mette, who originally lived with her father Morten and his partner, Erik. The English translation has the same pictures as the original Danish publication – not illustrations but black and white photographs of a real little girl and real young men. And it seems to have been these which caused such a furore when the book appeared in the 1980s. In a couple of them, the men appear to be naked, including in the photo of a pyjama-clad Jenny sitting in the arms of one of the men on their bed while the other man lies stretched out, reluctantly awakening. Here's the text that goes with this photo:

> Grownups always sleep such a lot.
> 'I am hungry,' Jenny whines miserably.
> 'Can't we have breakfast soon?'
> 'All right, all right,' says Martin, sitting up and rubbing his eyes. 'We will have breakfast then'.

> Eric sits up and yawns. 'Oh good, it's Saturday'…

Hansard of 2 December 1986 reports – in its deliciously deadpan way – an exchange between Harry Greenway and Angela Rumbold in the House of Commons:

Mr Greenway asked the Secretary of State for Education and Science what representations HMI (Her Majesty's Inspectorate) had received about the use by ILEA (the Inner London Education Authority) of the book and what action they are taking as a result.

Mrs Rumbold replied that HMI had received no direct representations and that

> My right hon. Friend has made clear to the ILEA his view that the book, which the authority acknowledges is unbalanced, has no place in any school whatever the circumstances, and that there can be no justification for retaining it in the authority's central loan collection.

And the ILEA masters – for so they were – in turn made it clear to the librarians working with the central loan collection that they were to remove the book from the shelves. This is where the story becomes interesting.

The librarians said they wouldn't. As an ILEA adviser on resources for educational equality, I was one of the librarians who put her job on the line for this banal little book. There wasn't anything better around in 1986 – this was the first children's book to challenge heteronormativity. It did so by illustrating a same-sex partnership and presenting it as unexceptional. Only it wasn't, of course – the gay partnership was the whole point of the book.

We librarians argued that the central library collection at County Hall was open only to adults – to ILEA staff. No child would have access to the books on those shelves. But we knew perfectly well that we were giving teachers and heads the chance to look at the book and maybe decide to buy a copy for their school. In short, we could be accused of promoting the book – which we were.

The irony was not lost on us that we, the guardians of quality literature for children, were risking our jobs for such a mediocre publication. But this was clearly a case for principle to prevail over substance, and the book was the only one around. So we dug in, the press had their fun, and then it all died down. The central collection copy of *Jenny* stayed on the shelves and 500 ILEA librarians all kept their jobs. So the story has a happy ending.

And when Margaret Thatcher finally abolished the Inner London Education Authority in 1990, ILEA staff would console themselves by saying that for her to swing her axe at the greatest education provider in the world, we must have got *some* things right. Looking back after nearly 20 years, I've no doubt that defending Jenny, Eric and Martin was one of them.

Some things do get better. For a start, the books for children published since Jenny blazed the trail are vivid and some are well written. They should beguile all children of the ages they target. What's important is that the *No Outsiders* project used them in class with all the children, whatever their family structures or their own emerging sexuality and that the books were enjoyed as good stories – or criticised according to literary criteria. That they normalise differences in sexualities was a bonus.

The book in your hands captures the feeling of involvement, of taking risks, that I remember from the Jenny affair. Most of us who defended the right of Jenny to remain on the shelves were straight so we thought of all the probably heterosexual children who needed to look at this book. Fine as far as it went, but only part of the story. In the volume you hold, you have the privilege of hearing not just from the straight members of the project, who echo my feelings all those years ago, but also the gay teachers and researchers, who take risks of a personal kind.

The accounts provided here by the adults who took part in the *No Outsiders* project are first and foremost deeply moving. But they are also inspirational for anyone who is striving for greater equality and fairness – especially for children. The joy of being a publisher is that I can bring work such as this lasting testament of the project of *No Outsiders*, of which this is the final volume in the trilogy, into the educational domain. Thank you all for putting yourselves on the line, and thank you, Renée DePalma and Elizabeth Atkinson, for enabling this unique and precious trilogy.

Gillian Klein
January 2010

Jenny lives with Eric and Martin by Susanne Bösche (Gay Man's Press, 1983)

Introducing the *No Outsiders* Project

Elizabeth A and Renée

Everyone is an insider, there are no outsiders – whatever their beliefs, whatever their colour, gender or sexuality. Archbishop Desmond Tutu, February, 2004

This is not a run-of-the-mill 'how to do it' book for primary teachers. It is a chronicle of one of the most daring and innovative projects to ever take place in primary schools: an attempt not simply to address homophobic bullying (something which should be on every school's agenda) but to *undo* homophobia at source, by challenging heteronormativity – the assumption that the world and everything in it is, and should be, based on a heterosexual model – and by challenging heterosexism – the privileging of heterosexual identities and relationships over all others. What is more, the project began in its second year to try to undo transphobia (discrimination against those who do not comply with gender norms) in the same way, by challenging the norms and stereotypes that keep girls and boys, men and women, fixed firmly in their gendered places.

> It doesn't really happen often, but sometimes around the school you hear people using 'gay' as an insult and it's just disgusting, 'cos it must be really offensive to some people who *are* gay.
> (Y6 pupil, North East)

We cannot claim to have reached our final goals: undoing deeply embedded norms around sexual orientation and gender expression in schools and in the wider community is a slow and continuous process, which will go on long after the publication of this book. But we have opened doors that cannot be closed again. We have shown that we can challenge these norms with children, colleagues, parents, governors and policy makers, and that this makes a noticeable difference to the lives of the people we work with – not only to those who identify, or might come to identify, as lesbian, gay, bisexual or transgender, but to all who, as a result of this work, begin to see the different colours of the kaleidoscope of identities of which we are a part.

So what did the *No Outsiders* project team do? Over a period of two and a half years, from September 2006 to March 2009, we worked with a growing team which eventually came to comprise 26 primary teacher-researchers across North East England, South West England, London and the Midlands, working in collaboration with nine university-based researchers at the University of Sunderland, the University of Exeter and the Institute of Education, University of London. The teacher-researcher team (each of whom worked extensively with colleagues in their own settings) comprised head teachers and class teachers, a university lecturer in primary education (who started with the project as a class teacher) and a local authority advisor for personal, social, health and citizenship education (PSHCE). Every practitioner member of the team is represented somewhere in this book. The sites in which the team members carried out their work, which involved children from pre-school to age 11, ranged from a tiny Church of England village school to a large suburban pre-school and playwork centre; from an almost all-white ex-mining village to urban schools serving communities representing a great many linguistic, cultural and religious backgrounds; from an urban school serving a largely Muslim community to another serving a largely Christian African-Caribbean community; and from schools where there were no known lesbian, gay, bisexual or transgender (LGBT) parents to schools where their presence was recognised and welcomed. Children in the project came from a whole spectrum of socio-economic backgrounds – in some cases with especially high levels of deprivation – and represented a range of special educational needs.

As a collaborative action research team, we set out to link practices and world-views that do not always reconcile neatly – theory and action, research and teaching, activism and academics – and together, we tried to address the following questions, which emerged as the project developed:

■ What are the key factors that a) facilitate and b) constrain LGBT equalities work in primary schools?

I was a pupil at my middle school when I decided that gay was the last thing I wanted to be. I was a 'spare child' at lunchtime. Being a spare child at lunchtime meant that you didn't have a table to sit at. At the beginning of the year we were sorted into groups of six, with two older children who were the servers. Some of us who weren't very popular didn't get into a group of six. This meant that at the beginning of lunchtime every single day, we had to go and stand at the front of the dining room while everyone said grace, and then we would fill in the spaces, because of course there were always children off. This became a trauma, an absolute trauma, because *every day* I'd be looking round the classroom wondering, 'Who's off? Can I make friends with so-and-so, is there a space at their table?' The morning was dominated with getting sorted for lunchtime. As I stood at the front, with everyone saying grace, I'd look around – 'Where shall I go, where shall I go?' I'd walk towards a space, and as I walked past people would say, 'Don't sit here poof, we don't want you on our table.' It wasn't very pleasant. Often people would say, 'You're a homo,' and I'd say, 'Oh yes, I'm a *homo sapiens*', which seemed like a smart comment – but it wasn't. At the end of that year I thought, 'The very last thing I ever want to or will be is gay.' I just think that if, at that point, someone had read a story where actually, people are quite happy being gay, that might have changed the next few years of my life. (Miles)

Issues to do with minorities aren't about minorities; they're about all of us. (Parent, North East)

■ How can sexual orientation and gender expression be addressed for children in ways that are relevant to their experience and growing understanding of personal identity, relationships and family diversity?

■ How can this work be extended across and beyond the curriculum, and are there specific curricular areas of particular value?

■ How can teachers' own positionings support or constrain classroom challenges to norms of sexuality and gender expression?

■ How do approaches to bisexual and transgender equalities mesh with approaches to lesbian and gay equalities?

■ What kinds of preparatory work are helpful, and how can the concerns of colleagues, parents and governors be addressed?

■ How can LGBT equality be approached in faith contexts?

■ How might the formation of a community of practice transform rather than reproduce existing practice?

■ How might the unsettling of certainties to be found in poststructuralist and queer theory inform classroom practice?

I think I would say to sceptics, I'm not sure what you're frightened of. There isn't anything to fear in one another, and I think we can be fearful of one another when we don't actually listen to one another, and when we react to stereotypes rather than reacting to human beings.
(Vicar, North East)

People are frightened of what they don't know, and that is where the problem starts.
(Grandmother, Midlands)

Needless to say, none of the answers to these questions are simple, and the path of exploring them has not been easy, but in this book you will find teachers' rich and varied responses to them, expressed through extracts from emails and postings from the team members' website, face to face conversations, chance remarks and anecdotes and images of the project's work. Apart from light editing for presentation, these conversations, exchanges, anecdotes and reflections have been kept as they originally appeared during the course of the project's work. We hope this will convey to readers the sense of excitement, discovery and sometimes danger which we as a team felt as the project explored new avenues.

Students, tutors and researchers in education, as well as practitioners wanting to explore more deeply the issues raised here, will find more studied responses to our research questions in our companion book, *Interrogating Heteronormativity in Primary Schools*, also published by Trentham. Both books are intended as openings to further conversations and explorations, rather than completed products: we are at the stage in challenging socially-embedded norms around sexual

Five year olds need to be taught that gay people exist. Some five year olds will already know this; there are children in our schools today who are being brought up by parents in a same sex relationship, and there are children who have gay uncles and aunts, gay brothers and sisters, gay grandparents. There are children living next door to gay people and children whose parents socialise with gay people. Gay people pop up on television programmes like Coronation Street, Hollyoaks and Emmerdale. Gay people are in fact everywhere.... except in the National Curriculum, and certainly not visibly in our schools.
(Andrew, introduction to Early Years Resource)

orientation and gender expression that we reached perhaps 40 years ago in challenging socially-embedded racism – and we still have a long way to go in both areas.

The project's work has been taken up by schools, local authorities, policy makers and equalities organisations across the UK, through workshops, presentations, mentoring programmes and professional development activities which have continued well beyond the end of the project's funded period. It has also been widely reported in the media – sometimes unkindly and sometimes enthusiastically – not only in the UK but across Europe and in the US, and across other countries including New Zealand, Canada, Mexico, Colombia and Brazil.

Whatever the stresses of being in the media spotlight – and there have been many – this has re-opened a vital public debate over what our children need to learn in school about the society they live in and the people who constitute it. And it has paved the way for a safer journey for those who follow us: you can read a story about a little girl with two mummies to a class of 4-year-olds without the sky falling in, your colleagues turning against you or your governing body calling for your dismissal; you can make a film of *King and King* or an opera of *And Tango Makes Three* without the world crashing down around your ears

> We've shown that it can be done, we've shown it doesn't have to be done to a template, that it can be done sensitively and contextually, and it doesn't have to be perfect each time. And that the teachers who've been involved in this want to carry on doing it after the project formally finishes. We've started something that people feel is worth carrying on with.
>
> *Nick, South West regional coordinator*

– you may receive praise, honour and gratitude for doing so! The teachers in this project were collectively awarded the British Educational Research Association/ Sage Publishers' *Research into Practice* award in 2008, and many of them have also received individual accolades and accreditation for their work. As leaders of the project, we have found working with them to be a privilege and an education. We hope, as their thoughts spring out from the pages of this book, that you will have the same experience.

A note on terminology

Many primary teachers told us about their anxiety over what terminology they should use in school when working on LGBT identities. They were afraid that actually using labels would somehow break rules and increase homophobic incidents. Teachers in the *No Outsiders* project have talked frankly with primary-age children about lesbian, gay, bisexual and transgender identities, as well as discussing with colleagues the relative merits of naming categories and queering education by refusing to box people's identities. For the comfort of teachers using this book, we provide some straightforward definitions below, with the reminder that it is in exploring what people (both children and adults) *think* lesbian, gay, bisexual and transgender mean, and the often unspoken negative connotations these terms carry, that much of the educational value of this work lies.

- ■ Lesbian: a woman who is emotionally and physically attracted to other women

- ■ Gay man: a man who is emotionally and physically attracted to other men

- ■ Bisexual: someone who is emotionally and physically attracted to both women and men.

- ■ Heterosexual: someone who is emotionally and physically attracted to people of the opposite sex from themselves. (For these four terms, it is useful to explore child-friendly ways of expressing them: for example, you might talking about people fancying or falling in love with other people)

- ■ Transperson/transgender person or gender variant person: someone whose gender assigned at birth (male or female) does not match or sit easily with their gendered sense of self. The terms 'transgender' and 'gender variant' are used to describe people who identify as outside of the gender binary of male or female, or people who live (with or without medical intervention) as a gender other than the one they were assigned at birth

- Trans man/transman: someone who was assigned female at birth but who identifies as a man or boy

- Trans woman/transwoman: someone who was assigned male at birth but identifies as a woman or girl

- Homophobia/biphobia/transphobia: these terms refer both to outright expressions of prejudice, dislike or distaste towards lesbian, gay, bisexual, trans and gender variant people and also to the silencing or ignoring by individuals and institutions of these people's identities or existence. Like institutional racism, institutional homophobia, biphobia and transphobia operate in schools as ways of marginalising non-heterosexual and non-gender normative identities

- Heterosexism: the way in which heterosexuality is assumed to be the only normal form, and therefore the superior form, of sexuality, and the

> I came to the project a year ago, and I thought, 'I'm not touching this with a barge pole! It's a no go area, it's gonna cause all sorts of problems!' Then my daughter came home and saw the project books and said, 'We can't have these in the house. People might think we're gay or something.' And I realised in that moment that at ten years old, she was already being bombarded with peer pressure; she'd already realised and made her mind up that gay is bad and we can't go there. That was when I realised that I had to get involved.
> (Roy, drama practitioner)

presumption that everyone is heterosexual unless otherwise stated. Heterosexism affects transgender and gender variant people as well as lesbian, gay and bisexual people in its insistence that the gender you were assigned at birth is the one that should determine your behaviour, who you fancy, and how you live your life.

Acknowledgements

From the outset, we have been supported by key educational bodies in the UK, who have given their vocal support to our work in ways which have sometimes brought their own organisations into the critical spotlight of the media. We would like to thank our four supporting organisations, the National Union of Teachers (NUT), the General Teaching Council for England (GTCE), *Schools Out* and Stonewall, as well as Jay Stewart of *Gendered Intelligence*, whose close involvement with our work has made him an honorary member of the project team. We are deeply indebted to Ros McNeil of the NUT, Sue Sanders of *Schools Out*, Lesley Saunders of the GTCE, and Chris Gibbons of Stonewall, who have been valued members of the project's advisory group, but who have gone well beyond this to support our work actively and publicly. The royalties from this book will be donated to *Schools Out*, in recognition of their tireless work over more than 30 years in support of LGBT educators, in gratitude to Sue Sanders, co-founder of *Schools Out* and LGBT History Month, and in memory of her co-founder, Paul Patrick, who died in May 2008. Finally, we would like to thank our funders, the Economic and Social Research Council (Project Reference RES-062-23-0095) and especially Alexandra Saxon (formerly of the Economic and Social Research Council and now of Research Councils UK) who has stood by us through thick and thin.

Photographs

The images of project work in this book have been kindly contributed by David Williams (williamsphoto.co.uk), Suited and Booted studios CIC (www.suitedand booted.org) and members of the *No Outsiders* project team. All images are from the project's work, but not necessarily from the setting being described in the text they accompany.

Contacts

For further information about the project, see our website, www.nooutsiders.sunderland.ac.uk

For information about professional development, including opportunities to work with members of the project team, please contact the project's diversity trainer, Mark Jennett: mark.jennett@btinternet.com.

For information and professional development on transgender awareness and support, please contact Jay Stewart at *Gendered Intelligence*: jay.stewart@ genderedintelligence.co.uk (www.genderedintelligence.co.uk).

For information about other support groups and organisations, see Chapter 8, Information and Resources.

Dedication

This book is dedicated to the memory of Katy Watson, author of *Spacegirl Pukes*, who died in August 2008. *Spacegirl* was a firm favourite with many of the children in the project. She will be sorely missed as an author, feminist activist, lesbian parent and member of *Out For Our Children*, a London-based organisation working for representation of LGBT identities in young children's education. We are delighted to have had the opportunity to support *Out For Our Children* in the production and distribution of hundreds of their *Real Families Rock* posters, which now grace the walls of numerous schools within and beyond the project.

No Outsiders is a ground breaking project which is contributing greatly to the teaching of equalities within primary schools. (Alexandra Saxon, Head of Communications at Research Councils UK)

Chapter 1

Why do it?

Promoting equality – or gay sex?
Mark

Mark Jennett, the project's diversity trainer (who worked with each of the project schools) outlines some of the key issues around the work of the No Outsiders *project team – especially the confusion between lesbian, gay and bisexual (LGB) sexual orientation and LGB sexual activity, and discusses how this confusion is the major cause of objections to LGB equalities work. He deliberately leaves the issue of transgender identity and gender expression to our other project consultant, Jay Stewart (see Chapters 5 and 7).*

LGB relationships are often seen as being mainly about sex. And since many people believe that sex has no place in the primary classroom, neither, in their view, do LGB people or their relationships. What they fail to perceive is that this obsession with what gay men and lesbians do in bed is an adult pre-occupation which children do not share.

A simple exercise will illustrate this. Think of all the names and words you hear used for lesbians or gay men. Get beyond the obvious 'poof' and 'lezzer' and many of them will be to do with sex – specifically anal or oral sex. Then ask yourself why the many straight people who enjoy these activities are rarely referred to as pillow biters, cock jockeys or rug munchers.

For many people, gay relationships mean first and foremost gay sex – not flirting, dating, falling in love, getting married,

raising children or any of the myriad activities gay people take part in just like their straight friends. Not everyone who thinks this is a dyed-in-the-wool homophobe (although the argument that children are too young to be learning about

> When I first heard about the project, I was slightly concerned as to how we would address sexualities equality in the primary school. And I think my fear was that somehow that was to do with sex . . . and – you know, how can we talk about that with children. But of course it wasn't to do with that at all. I think once we understood that, that made things a bit easier. But what really made things easy was that the children were completely unphased by it. (Sue E)

sex is often used by such individuals to justify their opposition to projects like *No Outsiders*). Rather, they are simply people who live in a heterosexist society which has largely reduced LGB people to a set of stereotypes ranging from the kind of sex they are perceived to have, to their tendency to be drawn to the arts (gay men), their fondness for short hair (lesbians) or their inability to commit to a single relationship (bisexuals).

In training sessions I sometimes tell people about a crush I had at the age of 8 on the man who delivered the bread in the small village where I was brought up. It is not often that people will insist nowadays that 'there are no gay people in our school' but even so, many people still assume all those gay people are adults – or at least teenagers. We smile when we see an 8 or 9 year old child clearly drawn to an adult of the opposite sex and talk indulgently about their having a 'crush' – and yet when we see a boy who is fond of a particular older male we call it hero worship. Maybe it is – or maybe he is just experiencing what I did – and what many children, whatever their eventual sexual orientation, will experience – a perfectly normal, perfectly healthy and rather touching little infatuation which has nothing to do with sex and everything to do with the process of growing up and learning about the kinds of relationships we will have as adults.

The point of this story is to illustrate how, when we talk about LGB relationships to children, they don't bring the same baggage with them that adults often do. When we read them a story about two princes who fall in love, they accept it for what it is – and don't think it has anything more to do with sex than the story of Cinderella and *her* prince. Yet by Key Stage 2 (age 7-11), many of the children in the project schools had already internalised the idea of being gay as something wrong or to be laughed at, whereas the younger children had no such preconceptions. Indeed many little boys and girls are delighted by the idea that they could marry someone of the same gender if they wanted to or think of children with two dads as being quite lucky – after all, some people don't even have one.

Teachers often express concerns about whether children might ask about how Spacegirl, the eponymous heroine of *Spacegirl Pukes* (one of the books teachers used in the project schools), came to live with her two mums – and whether this

> Mark came in and he said, you know, you shouldn't be scared, you're just teaching the facts. And I think from then on that was like 'Oh! Actually, yeah I *am* just teaching them the facts. (Jon)

might lead to questions about sex and how LGB people 'have babies'. In fact this seldom happens. When it does it is actually an opportunity to talk about the many different ways parents – whatever their sexual orientation – have children, be it through procreating, adoption, fostering, or falling in love with a partner who already has children, and about how factors like divorce, separation and bereavement contribute to the formation of extended families. How often do children ask (or adults worry) about where the children in stories 'come from' when they have heterosexual parents? It's no different when the parents happen to be of the same gender.

One teacher recounted an incident which took place after she talked with her class about a picture in *Spacegirl Pukes* which shows a poorly Spacegirl tucked up in bed with her equally sickly mummies. A little girl in the class raised her hand to confirm that her mummies – like the ones in the story – shared a bedroom. Several other hands went up and the teacher – far from needing to address questions ranging from the details of IVF treatment to lesbian sex – was regaled with tales of how 'my mum shares a bedroom with my dad', 'I share a bedroom with my sister' and 'I used to share a bedroom with my brother but we've moved to a bigger house so I've got my own room now'. Again – nothing to do

Left: Mark Jennet working with pupils in a project school

with sex and everything to do with the domestic arrangements that most children recognise.

Those against ...

Just to illustrate adults' obsession with sexual activity, one of the small minority of parents who remained implacably opposed to any mention of same sex relationships in the classroom announced triumphantly that it was actually impossible to know whether Roy and Silo (the two penguin fathers in *And Tango Makes Three*) were gay since we didn't know what kind of sex they were having. It was hard not to revel in pointing out that a) we rarely (if ever) know what kind of sex the characters in children's books are having but we still generally assume that they are heterosexual and b) more to the point, we know that Roy and Silo are gay because, early in the story, we learn that they do all the things that the other penguin couples do to show their affection for each other so the zookeeper realises that 'they must be in love'.

There is a more serious point to this story. Objections to the discussion of LGB relationships – or at least to their presentation as 'normal' and 'acceptable' – are a form of homophobia. But those who voice such objections will vehemently deny they are homophobic, and this sometimes inhibits teachers from responding to these often strongly expressed challenges. It is important for teachers to remember that talking about LGB relationships, far from being the same as talking about LGB sex, is simply part of the work schools already do to introduce children to a wide range of people and family structures – and many children already have LGB people amongst their extended families anyway. And it is difficult to challenge homophobic bullying effectively without challenging the idea that there is something wrong about being LGB. This in turn is difficult to do without talking about LGB relationships in a way that children can relate to in the same way as they can to heterosexual ones – e.g. in terms of being parents, falling in love or getting married. Since anyone who is unwilling to acknowledge their own homophobia could never be seen to condone homophobic bullying ... well, you can see where I'm going with this.

> I wouldn't go and ask them if we can teach Islam, I wouldn't go and ask them whether I can teach them about a different denomination of Christianity, I wouldn't go and ask them if I was going to teach about age or explore gender so why would I have to say something about this? I wouldn't deny it but we just do it. (Jo)

All these points can be useful counters when people object to any discussion of LGB identities in the primary classroom. If we put the ball back in their court and ask them what the problem is, sooner or later they will fall over their own logic. One woman could offer no reason for her vehement and aggressive objection to the *No Outsiders* project other than her Christian faith. When told that some of the teachers leading the work were themselves people of faith, she declared that they 'were not proper Christians': a view to which they strongly objected.

Until this point, other parents and staff had felt they needed to accommodate her views in some way, but her comments made it clear that she would only be satisfied if they gave in completely and stopped any discussion of LGB relationships. Since this would have implied that the school did not value the LGB members of its community – and particularly the children at the school who had LGB parents – equally, they simply informed her that the work would be going ahead – saving themselves a lot more time and distress.

In sessions I ran with parents and governors, opponents would occasionally make comments which, had they been said about any other minority, would have drawn gasps from the rest of the room. That such remarks didn't have this effect

did not mean others agreed with them – the teachers' responses to the project ranged from wild enthusiasm to cautious acceptance – but rather that people feel less confident about challenging homophobia than they do racism, say, or prejudice about disability. In situations like these, directly challenging such comments can be less constructive than asking them why they feel that children need to be protected from LGB people, and how a school can be inclusive, safe and welcoming for all children if those with same sex parents, LGB relations or family friends – or children who might one day identify as LGB – don't see themselves and their lives reflected and endorsed in school like their peers are. You might not convince them but you expose their homophobia for what it is, which makes it easier for people who are afraid to challenge such views to come out in support of the work and vote the opponents down. And when they see what the work actually entails and where it leads – to greater acceptance of difference,

> As it's antibullying week, upper key stage 2 were reading out poems they'd written. Year 6's were based on Martin Luther King's *I have a dream* and one girl (who has two mums) said she has a dream that people become tolerant of homosexuality. (Katherine)

a notion of diverse families, a better understanding of why homophobic bullying or language is hurtful – some of those opponents might even come on board themselves.

Justifying the work...

So, perhaps inevitably, we sometimes have to spend as much time and energy battling the negative as we do promoting the positive. But we should not anticipate objections before they arise. I used to advocate holding meetings to tell parents about work on challenging homophobia but now I am not so sure. Would we feel the need to draw their attention to work we did on racism, sexism or other forms of discrimination? Don't we actually risk *creating* the impression that work on promoting LGBT equalities is controversial and challenging? This isn't SRE (Sex and Relationships Education) – it's simply a development of the work that schools are already doing on difference, diversity, families and relationships. Parents have no automatic right to withdraw their children so why do we need to tell them – to warn them – even before we begin? Perhaps we fear they might object on the grounds of faith – but aren't relationships between people who haven't been married in the eyes of their God also perceived by some as unacceptable? Yet would we hesitate to endorse the validity of single parent families, unmarried or divorced parents?

Maybe sometimes we should go ahead – confident of our reasons for talking to children about LGB relationships – and see what happens.

The books

The need to justify discussion of LGB relationships explains the limitations of some of the books that formed the basis of much of the teaching in *No Outsiders* schools. Interestingly, most of the 'gay' characters are coupled and usually presented as parents. These parents are also invariably and sometimes unrealistically 'good' – even though in many books for quite young children parents are not always present or are too busy with their own concerns to notice their children's problems. The team struggled to find books in which the characters are really comfortable with their specialness – *The Sissy Duckling* and *The Paper Bag Princess* are notable exceptions. We never found a book where lesbian mums weren't poised ready with a nutritious meal when junior came home or who were sometimes too busy to help their daughter with her homework.

Many teachers in the project said they were uncomfortable with the book *Daddy's Roommate* because of the big age difference between the gay dads and because they were shown sharing a bathroom and bedroom -familiar images

in stories about heterosexual parents – which they felt sexualised their relationship too much. By contrast few if any objected to the image of a naked and (presumably) heterosexual couple cavorting in the pages of a Babette Cole picture book under the caption 'Why do Mummy and Daddy lock me out of their bedroom?' The fact that *And Tango Makes Three*'s Roy and Silo are animals and not humans possibly makes them less real and therefore less potentially sexualised. This perhaps partly explains why this was by far the most popular book with the adults on the project.

Interestingly, while many of the books aim to normalise gay parents in rather outdated ways, most of the stories undermine this by being all about the gay parents and their children – as though their very existence is story enough. The titles: *Asha's Mums, Heather Has Two Mommies, If I Had A Hundred Mummies, Molly's Family, Daddy's Roommate*, say it all. Rarely are books, except some of those for very young children, just about having a mum and a dad. Amongst the books we found about same sex parents, only *Spacegirl's* mums are incidental to rather than the focus of the story in the same way as fictional heterosexual parents. When children's books show them in the background or feature lesbian mums who are so busy at work they feed their children

My daughter's father is gay ... I'm also a disabled woman and my child has an impairment, so I know what it's like to be un/misrepresented and on the outside. I want her to be able to go to school and see all of us represented wherever she turns, including in the books she is learning to read. And I want her friends, their parents and the teachers to see us represented so they begin to realise how very ordinary our different-ness is. (Email from 'a single mother, straight woman' in the UK)

I realized I was gay when I was only 11. My only exposures were gay jokes at school and constant reminders of how any homosexual would die for the sin of their 'unnatural' desires alone. This was a very, very dark time in my life. If I had read those children's books, if I knew that maybe someone close to me understood, my life would have been completely different. (Email from 'an 18-year-old homosexual' in Canada)

Nobody's heart really seems to be into homophobia any more. (Zoë Williams, writing for *The Guardian*)

How I wish it were true that homophobia is a thing of the past. I want a world that is safe for my son, where his family is not regarded as weird. (Letter to T*he Guardian*)

fast food, this may be the sign that LGB parents and relationships are at last accepted.

It is significant that one of the images most often reproduced in the press when the project was discussed – whether positively and negatively – was the last page of *King and King*. It shows the two princes kissing, with a large heart covering their mouths. Did the authors mean to stress the princes' love or was it a kind of unconscious fig leaf, meant to desexualise their union by concealing their lips? Either way, it seems to represent what the project's detractors most feared. Perhaps it's not gay sex that they want to protect children from but gay love. Showing gay people in love puts their relationships on a par with straight ones and makes them something we can all relate to, regardless of our own sexual orientation or even whether we understand what having a sexual orientation might imply. By stressing the love in LGB relationships, do we offend our homophobic critics most of all? But that, children, is a whole other story...

UK Government Legislation, Guidance and Support
Elizabeth A, Mark and Renée

This is where we are heading, we are heading to obey the law of the land. But we've got a journey to travel and let's travel together. (Head teacher, South West)

UK Legislation

2003: The repeal in 2003 in England (2000 in Scotland) of Section 28 of the 1988 Local Government Act (which banned Local Education Authorities from 'the promotion of homosexuality as a pretended family relationship') paves the way for further legislation in relation to LGBT equalities.

2003: The Employment Equality (Sexual Orientation) Regulations require schools to ensure that LGB employees are not subject to direct or indirect discrimination. Indirect discrimination includes, for example, experiencing unchallenged negative references to LGB people, whether or not they relate to the individual concerned.

2004: The introduction of *Every Child Matters* under the Children Act requires Local Authorities to make provision for 'every child, *whatever their background or circumstances* to have the support they need to be healthy, stay safe, enjoy and achieve, make a positive contribution and achieve economic well-being'. This includes children with LGBT family members and children who grow up to identify as LGBT. *Every Child Matters* also requires that young people 'feel safe from bullying and discrimination' and 'choose not to bully or discriminate'.

2005: The Civil Partnership Act is passed. The relationships of many LGB parents now enjoy similar legal status to those of married heterosexual couples. This advance places an onus on schools to consciously recognise families based on same-sex partnerships, and to discuss these families as confidently as they do others.

2006: The Education and Inspections Act places a duty on Ofsted (Office for Standards in Education) inspectors to ensure that schools proactively prevent all forms of bullying, and the Ofsted framework for inspections incorporates a specific reference to homophobic incidents. Schools also have a duty to promote the well-being of pupils. This would include pupils with LGBT family members, and those who identify as LGBT or who might do in future.

2006: The Equality Act outlaws discrimination on the grounds of sexual orientation in the provision of goods and services. This means, for example, that a pupil could not be refused entry to a school on the grounds that they were, or were thought to be, LGB or because they had LGB parents. The School Admissions Code also prohibits discrimination on the basis of a pupil's or parent's sexual orientation. By inference, LGB parents should feel as welcome as any other parents in the school.

2007: The Gender Equality Duty, introduced as part of the implementation of the 2006 Equality Act, requires schools to promote gender equality in the same way as they do race and disability equality. The Equal Opportunities Commission (now part of the Equalities and Human Rights Commission) makes it clear in their guidance to schools that to do this without addressing homophobia, and its links with sexism, would be impossible. The duty includes promoting inclusion for children who do not conform to traditional gender norms – and they note that children who are seen by their peers to break gender norms are frequently subject to homophobic bullying.

2009: The new Equality Bill, *A Fairer Future*, published in April 2009 paves the way for the introduction of a single Equality Act, which will tackle disadvantage and discrimination based on race, gender, disability, age, sexual orientation, religion or belief, affirming sexual orientation and gender as key equalities areas and imposing a single equality duty on all public bodies to proactively promote equality of opportunity for all.

Government guidance and support

Note: at the time of going to press, the name of the government department dealing with primary education was the Department for Children, Schools and Families. Over the years, however, primary education has been the remit of departments with various titles.

2000: The Department for Education and Skills' (DfES) guidance on Sex and Relationships Education includes the recognition of diversity in family relationships, the need to ensure that education about relationships is relevant to all young people regardless of their emerging sexual orientation and that teachers should be able to deal honestly and sensitively with sexual orientation.

2004: The joint publication by the DfES and the Department of Health of *Stand Up For Us*, introduced to coincide with the launch of National Anti-Bullying Week in November, illustrates how to develop a whole school approach to addressing homophobia using the Healthy Schools framework.

2005: The Behaviour and Attendance and SEAL (Social and Emotional Aspects of Learning) strands of the DfES' Primary National Strategy suggest a proactive approach to curricular inclusion, specifically listing gender and sexual orientation as key areas.

I hope, in school, that we've just put the LGBT equality strand on the maps. (Sue E)

2005: The DfES supports the launch by *Schools Out* of LGBT History Month, implying a commitment not just to combating the effects of homophobia in schools and elsewhere, but to a proactive policy of inclusion for LGBT in the curriculum.

2005: Ofsted and the DfES join Stonewall's *Education for All* coalition, a three-year campaign to eradicate homophobic bullying in schools.

2007: The Department for Children, Schools and Families (DCSF) incorporates guidance on homophobic bullying into their *Safe to Learn* anti-bullying materials, including guidance on proactive approaches in the primary schools.

2008: The Home Office publishes guidance on *Combating Transphobic Bullying in Schools* which emphasises that for some pre-pubertal children, regardless of whether or not they choose gender reassignment in later life, 'the need to express gender variance in behaviour and experience is very powerful' (p11).

Offenders of the world

Black, White or Pink
Everyone's different!
Many people think,
Whether you're Lesbian or Gay,
No one should have anything to say,
Which will offend you in any way!

Racism is a thing, which will never be forgot,
Hurting you inside a lot,
Like a burning hot volcano,
Which will never go away,
Why are people getting hurt like this?
I think to myself today,
Why…

If you are Lesbian or Gay
And it is the way you feel,
You should be proud to say,
'I am Gay'
– Don't hide away,
Despite everything that happens,
Which offends you in many ways,
Lesbian if you are,
Don't hang far,
Lesbian or Gay.

(Year 6 pupil, North East)

Chapter 2

Inspirations and openings

In Chapters 2 to 6, project team members present their own experiences of No Outsiders work, drawing on presentations, emails, conversations and web postings during the course of the project, and reflecting back on their experience as a whole. For a full list of the children's books and other project resources referred to in these pages, see Chapter 8.

Focus on Families in an After School Art Club *Miles*

Taken from a presentation to local educators, policy makers and interest groups.

I thought, 'I'll run an art club just like Kate did [see Chapters 3 and 7 for descriptions of Kate's work] and we'll look at the family.' I opened it up to everybody, but also had a little bit of targeting of families within the school. The school I'm at has more same sex parents than many of the schools in the city, so we had an interesting cross section, including quite a few children from same-sex families. We looked at what a family was, starting at the beginning with the words you associate with family. We had words like 'loving', 'caring', as you'd expect, but also things like 'all different', 'weird' and 'sticky' – a whole range of phrases.

Many of the children in our school are not in what we'd call conventional families. If you look at any class in our school, there's a whole host of different family arrangements: children with single parents, some with same-sex parents, some looked after by grandparents, some fostered, some adopted. There isn't a 'normal' in our school. But I think a lot of the children still feel that they *should* be from something normal, or have a desire to be from what they consider to be normal. Until they come to school they are used to their family being a normal family – suddenly they're aware that in some people's eyes, it's not.

We went on in our project to start looking at portraits of families. We worked with a local artist and looked at a pile of pictures I tracked down of different kinds of families, including one of *my* family (two

I started off the project feeling very proud and relieved to be involved: here at last was something I needed to be part of, mostly to ensure that no child I ever came into contact with went through what I went through in primary and secondary school. More and more as the project has developed, this has become a driving force in continuing what I'm doing; this has often kept me going in the face of any adversity and prejudice that has reared its ugly head. (John)

dads and two children). It was always an issue for me – the extent to which I talked about myself, because the project was never about turning children gay – it was about making them aware of difference.

There were three reasons why I felt this was important. We do have children from same-sex families, and I *do* want them to feel included. We do have children who will start to identify themselves as gay or lesbian. However there are also many people who come from quite intolerant families. And this might be the only chance in their life where somebody says, 'there are other ways of living'. We are not trying to turn those people gay but just to start some conversations, because children form their opinions very early on, and if we don't start talking about it now, it may be too late.

'I've got two gay dads and I've got two lesbian mums as well. That's the kind of wedding that my family would have.' (Year 2 pupil)

Using the Project Books in School
Andi

The books were there, people have talked about it, people have asked me things. But I didn't want to say, 'And now you will have your forty five minutes of gayness every week.' (Miles)

Web posting to the project team:
One of the teachers has taken a couple of books to have judgement passed on them by a 'gay friend' – well if he 'judges them' to be inappropriate, oh dear, what am I to do? The gay friend took the books into work (he's a social worker) and some of his colleagues (single, married, gay etc) made comments too. Then one of his colleagues took the books home to read with her kids, and her partner looked at them and decided he would take them to his work (he's a nurse) to ask for comments. I had no idea where the books were heading ...

Emails to Elizabeth B (research assistant)
1 March
Just to let you know that I'm going to use one of *our* books tomorrow in class – we are covering the SEAL (Social and Emotional Aspects of Learning) topic 'Good to be me' – which is about a mouse having a special strength to save the strong fearful lion. Also in Literacy we are doing the fairy tale *Cinderella* this and next week. Today I was thumbing through the project books and I was just wondering how to move the situation on, and decided there and then to use one of the books and just deal with stuff as and when it happens – if anything does happen! I'm just going to use it in the going home, calming down time to just look at other families as different as Cinderella's. Of course, I will discuss the different families we all have in our class beforehand. I think it will be very interesting!

2 March
It went well. As with any other circle time I reinforced the rules, then we discussed our families. I started off, then it went round: 'My family is special because I have a rabbit' etc. I said I had two cats, two sons and a grandson. I read the story *And Tango Makes Three* and they were all engrossed, 'oohing' and 'aahing' in the right places. One boy just said, 'Aah, that's nice, two dads'. Another said, 'It's two boys,' but nothing else really. One little girl who had been out of the room during the story came back in time for the last two pages (when Tango is shown to the public) and as I finished, I asked if anyone would tell her

the beginning of the story. One of the pupils (who has special educational needs) said, 'It's in a big city. It's about two boy penguins, and an egg that needed to be saved.' Nothing else. So then I asked what they thought of the story, and one child said, 'I think they would be very, very happy if they had another egg and got another baby. Then there'd be twins and each boy could look after one each.' (We do have twins in my class.) But that was it, no comments or anything really. I knew it would be ok. I'm going to do this every Friday until all the books are used up!

10 March

Read *Asha's Mums* yesterday. Comments: 'Yes, you can have two mums: I have two mums,' from a girl whose parents have split up and are with other partners (not LGBT that I know of). Others in the class agreed, with lots saying, 'I have two nanas and two dads, two mams,' etc. Another said, 'I have a step mam and a real mam.' They all agreed you can have two mams. Another commented on the use of black and white and colour illustrations. No one commented on the fact that there were two mums of the same sex living together. My next move I think is to start introducing that the story is actually about two women who love each other and live together – and see what happens ... !

Of course there are children in schools that have two mums or two dads, just as there are children in schools who have no mum or dad. It seemed stupid that we didn't have books depicting this, when we had so many other books which showed various types of family. (Rachael)

Year 1 pupil's guided writing

'Not doing much' – or changing the world?

Boni

Time and again, as we talked to teachers around the country about their involvement in the project, they would say, 'I'm really not doing much, you know'. Yet it became increasingly obvious that it was through the little things, the day-to-day shifts in thinking, that big changes were taking place. Below are some extracts from two conversations between Boni, Renée and Elizabeth A, exploring some of the ways this was happening in Boni's multicultural school community.

Boni: It's going OK. I still suffer this guilt that I'm not really doing anything, then I think, 'Don't be daft,' because we are doing quite a lot really. Just bedding it in and staying with it.

Elizabeth: You know, I don't think we've yet spoken to any member of the project who hasn't said what you've just said.

Boni: But I feel I should introduce a whole marvellous change of the world thing.

Elizabeth: Well, you have, you are! You know, we are all beating ourselves up all the time but this is all so crazy, you know: everything that has happened, whether it's somebody saying one sentence to a colleague in a staffroom, writing a scheme

> I took six children to the swimming pool on Friday, and as I was standing outside the changing room I heard one boy say, 'Last one out of the changing room is gay.' I said, 'It's interesting that the speed it takes you to get changed actually affects your sexuality. Can you explain that?' (Miles)

of work or reading a story, it's changing the world all the time.

Boni: Next year I want to drill down a bit more, get a bit more in touch with what kids are thinking and their responses. And I want it to be a bit more out there. This year, being the head, a lot of it has been about setting the ground, treading carefully, watching out. I want to take the 6-week module on sexualities Andrew [another project teacher] has done and deliver it here with Year 6 in a team teaching situation. And we'll have his emotional literacy materials as a full strand in our PSHCE (personal, social, health and citizenship education) every term.

Using the project books in the eye of the media storm ...

Renée: I have to say that I was really surprised that you chose the week of the media whirlwind to read *And Tango Makes Three.*

Boni: Well, I did and I didn't: it was all planned beforehand. When we looked at what assembly themes we would have last term, we identified one week that was families and one week that was parents and carers. So there was my vehicle; and it just happened that it coincided with the media coverage of the project. I read *Heather Has Two Mummies* and then *Tango* in three assemblies and I just went for it. And do you know, there was ... nothing. It was like, 'Hello, did anybody hear me read these stories?' But I got very panicky when it all came out in the media, and I thought, 'I am going to have to withdraw from the project because we are going to be identified'. I couldn't sleep. I thought, 'That's it, my job's on the line'. But Annie (who is PSHE advisor for the borough, as well as being a project teacher) went to the Director, made sure that everybody knew and said it's OK. I mean, this is a fantastic borough for equalities; they couldn't *not* support it, could they?

I fronted with *Tango Makes Three*: 'This is a true story' – and the comment that came back was that the kids thought the zoo keeper was so kind. You know, forget the two male penguins ... ! So I thought, 'I wonder if they don't really see it'. But another child said, 'It's rather unusual, though, to have two males'. And I did actually say in front of the whole school, 'You can have two male parents, two female parents, that's OK, isn't it?' And she went, 'Oh yes'. And I just left it there.

Year 1 pupil's writing for class book

Working outside our comfort zones
Judy

At the end of the first year, Judy shared her experiences with an audience of education professionals in her Local Authority:

Through being in the project I've had to challenge my own perceptions, and I've come to marry my professional self with my personal self in dealing with the issues that have been raised. Getting involved in the project took me out of my comfort zone in talking about sexuality and gender issues. I'm not big on belly-button searching: I'm not looking for me to change. I've taken on the role of the professional person delivering what is, by rights, the education of all children, but I still see these issues as uncomfortable. And if parents are negative, if they don't like what's going on in school, that's going to reflect on the teacher and the school. Are we really prepared to marginalise ourselves in the pursuit of education for sexualities equality?

I've never considered myself homophobic in any kind of situation, but I've never had to bring it into my professional life. I can sit round a table and have a drink with my mates in the pub and have a chat with my gay brother and my son who is at the moment exploring his sexuality, but I've never had to bring it into a professional forum, so to me that was a huge step. Just saying the words was difficult – I'm taking a bit of a risk sharing this with you, but I felt uncomfortable at the start of the training because I didn't know what Mark was going to say. He knew exactly what boundaries he was going to break down, but I was on the receiving end, and I'm thinking, 'Oh God, what is he going to say now; oh God, he's going to say … ' and it conjured up all sort of images of things that I was really uncomfortable with. And towards the end of the session he said, 'OK, let's address the prejudice as it is.' He just got right to the point.

People define gay men in terms of the sexual activities they imagine them to be engaging in, they seem to have an image of gay men as 'shagging each other up the arse all day long.' We need to recognise this as our own prejudice and move on. And I thought, 'Oh, OK, I feel much better now,' and the shock was gone, because that is people's perception, and I kind of moved on and thought, 'OK, right, that's the worst it's going to get. Now what's the project about?'

17

Chapter 3

A kaleidoscope of approaches

No Outsiders at Nursery Level
Jade

I work in a 52-place nursery which provides full day care for young children aged 3 months to 5 years and pre-school for 3 and 4 year olds. We are based on the outskirts of London in an area that is mainly white working class. Our nursery ethos defines inclusion as central to our practice and we have a robust and detailed inclusion policy which addresses areas of inclusion including disability, mental health, age, LGBT inclusion, race and gender. Ours was the only early years provision in *No Outsiders*, and this itself was a challenge. How do you introduce LGBT equality to very young children without giving parents and carers the wrong impression? The answer lay in our already existing approach.

Because our children are so young, we chose not to do a single focused project around LGBT equality. Instead, we used materials from the project such as storybooks and posters and wove them into the fabric of our everyday work. We looked closely at our practice with the children, focusing particularly on gender-aware language and gender stereotypes. My main concern as centre manager and lead practitioner on the project in our setting was that LGBT equality should become a part of everyday practice rather than a tokenistic dip into an area of inclusion that is still difficult for people to accept. The need for a subtle yet explicit approach was obvious from the outset.

In any early years setting, there is a constant dialogue between parents and carers and the nursery provider. The approach to early years education is viewed as a partnership between parents and carers and the nursery, and it is vital that trust forms the foundation of that

Dressing up in an Early Years centre

relationship. After all, parents have a right to know what their children are learning. I wanted them to understand fully what it means for us to be an inclusive setting that values all families, including those made up of lesbian, gay, bisexual and transgender people. I discussed our inclusion policy with families during induction, drawing attention to resources such as storybooks and posters that explore different families. The responses I received varied from very positive to very negative. One parent who works as a police officer in the local area said:

> I'm really glad that you're doing this. So much hate crime goes on through lack of awareness and understanding about difference. Children need to learn about difference from a young age in a way that makes it OK. I am totally fine with that.

Another parent thought otherwise:

> This changes things for me. I am a Christian and my religion says that homosexuality is wrong. I would not be comfortable with my child thinking it is OK for two men to be together in the same way as a man and a woman.

I challenged her argument and suggested that Christianity does not assume that homosexuality is wrong. I explained that a number of Christians were involved in the project and pointed out that the

underlying message in Christianity is love thy neighbour. The parent replied: 'My husband is not a Christian but I think he would have an even bigger problem with it than I do'. I suggested that possibly religion was not the reason for their prejudice and was being used as a 'get out of jail free' card. Needless to say, I did not see this parent again.

I have had good comments and bad, I have had some honest and open ongoing dialogues with parents about LGBT equality. During an open session, one father noticed the Real Families Rock poster from *Out For Our Children*, featuring 'dad's partner Roy' on the wall in reception. He looked at me and said, 'What's this then?' I reminded him of our inclusion policy and our involvement in the project. He clearly wanted to talk and we started the first of many interesting conversations. His first question was 'why are you doing this?' His initial feelings were that it was not right to display the poster to children at such a young age, and that having gay parents was the worst case scenario for any child. I asked him if he thought this was really so. Is a home where a child is loved and cared for by gay parents worse than a home, for argument's sake, where a child witnesses her mother being beaten by her father every day?

I felt it was important that he understood the intention behind the project. I

explained that we are not advertising or advocating homosexuality to young children. Neither are we and shoving it in their faces. We are saying to children that some children have a mum and a dad and some children have two mummies or two daddies. By being honest with children and explaining about different types of family, we are trying to reduce homophobic bullying and discrimination later in life. I explained that whilst the project is about embracing difference, for children in the early years, the emphasis is on similarities more than differences, using *Spacegirl Pukes* to illustrate my point. This story is not about a little girl having two mummies. It is about a little girl flying in a space rocket, who gets a tummy bug before she flies and is looked after by her two mummies. Children who have been cared for by their parents when they are ill can easily relate to this.

Towards the end of the conversation, the dad was beginning to consider some of my arguments and became willing to learn more about the project and the way we were using the materials. He realised that his views were not necessarily those of the majority and were in part a fear of the unknown. It became evident that many of his beliefs around gay parents were based on stereotypes, and the formation of pejorative stereotypes amongst young children is exactly what we are working against at the nursery. We know that young children inherit attitudes and beliefs from their parents and, to judge from my observations, this begins to take effect at around pre-school age through the display of gender stereotypes in everyday play.

For us, working against stereotyping has probably been the focus of the project. We know that for children in their early years the learning environment is crucial. Young children need to be stimulated to question the world around them and begin to form ideas. Just by provoking curiosity around an object or a picture and asking children what they think about something can challenge them enough to question the common stereotypes. For example, we might say to a child when we are looking at a picture in a storybook, 'This person has short hair. Do you think it is a girl or a boy?' or, 'This person is playing with baby dolls. Do girls or boys do that?' This kind of questioning enables children to use their imagination and draw on their own experience in response. And it encourages them to apply skills of reasoning and change their views accordingly.

My agenda was then, and still is, to normalise lesbian, gay, bisexual and transgender families and ensure that every person coming to the early years centre feels welcomed and valued. (Jade)

We developed critical thinking through discussion and also used animal puppets in a similar way to persona dolls to challenge common stereotypes. For example, one of our puppets, called Mikey Monkey, is in fact a girl. Mikey is short for Michaela and she likes to do things like running and playing tricks on people. Her favourite TV programme is Doctor Who and she also likes to play dressing up and cooking. We invented Mikey Monkey because we noticed that many of the children were beginning to conform to gender stereotypes in their play. The boys were not letting the girls play rough and tumble and both girls and boys were taking on traditional gender roles during domestic play.

A whole school approach to equalities work
Sue K

The process began with an audit, using the Centre for Studies in Inclusive Education's *Index for Inclusion* materials, staff, parent/carer and pupil questionnaires and surveys. An inclusion steering group, including community representation, was established and priorities identified. Key messages to all staff, led by the senior leadership team, included the following:

■ Inclusion is a human rights issue: the right to education, the right to have your life experiences represented positively and the right to be free from discrimination

■ Inclusion is a priority in our school

■ Inclusion requires a never-ending process of changing cultures, policies and practices

■ We must never underestimate our role in helping to create a more just society

■ Everyone needs to feel welcome in our school

The school then developed a set of school values, summarised in six terms: Respect, Unity, Creativity, Spirituality, Cooperation and Perseverance. We did values work with the staff initially, then with parents and carers and then with the children. There was ownership of and commitment to these values, which supported what we were trying to do in equalities. We shared the key inclusion messages with parents and carers and also with the children.

At whole school assemblies, we launched the school values, focusing on one of the values each week. We acknowledged the children who demonstrated the chosen value, and linked each value to a values-based curriculum. The values-based curriculum was incorporated into all classroom practice so that learning objectives always included one value and success was measured both in terms of the learning objective and of who had demonstrated the value identified for that session or day.

Once the ethos was established and everyone was on board we were able to start implementing our priorities for inclusion. We devoted a professional development day to discussing equalities legislation, links to the curriculum and feelings about doing this sort of work. We focused first on race and disability equality. We provided interpreters for School Meal Supervisory Assistants whose English was not fluent and they were hugely grateful for the opportunity to discuss these issues in their home language. It was important to acknowledge people's different starting points and we ensured that everyone knew it was alright to make mistakes or say the 'wrong thing'. The key message that came out of the professional development day was that equalities work with children was about human rights. One member of staff came to me the next day and thanked me for the day, saying that it had changed her as a person.

Following this professional development day, staff agreed to plan one equalities curriculum activity each. This had to be a manageable task so we could come back as a group and evaluate what we had done and talk about our feelings about it. Some of the activities are discussed below. All the staff were extremely positive and as a result an 'equalities links' column was incorporated into the medium term planning proforma. It was important that work around disability, race and gender equality, and later work challenging homophobia, was integrated into our planning and not just part of stand-alone PSHE sessions or issue based teaching.

Specific curriculum areas and equalities links

Literacy

Children looked at examples of advertisements before writing or designing their own. The adverts included some from disabled people's magazines. We discussed the need for the children's own adverts to reach as wide a section of the community as possible and how to achieve this. The teaching resources included leaflets from EACH (Educational Action Challenging Homophobia) and DISEED (Disability Equality in Education). We collected leaflets from the community so that as many groups as possible were represented. Children designed their own leaflets to reach the widest possible audience.

We used role model authors as a literacy focus. We had already featured Oscar Wilde as a role model of the week for choosing to be true to himself, and we paid particular attention to his statement: 'It is better to be hated for who you are than loved for who you are not'. We spent time discussing what he meant and how his life was affected – being imprisoned for being gay – and what the implications might be for us. Children read some of his stories in class and read biographies and autobiographies about different people. We included books about civil rights leaders and included Harvey Milk. Children wrote their autobiographies but also did writing about how they would like to improve the world, starting with Martin Luther King's 'I have a dream', with which they were already familiar.

In work on traditional tales, teachers used books such as *King and King* and alternative versions of traditional tales to challenge stereotypes relating to disability, gender and sexual orientation and particularly the dearth of non-heterosexual characters in children's books. We constantly returned to the key principle that everyone should have their experiences reflected. We had a child who was open about having two mums so the idea of same sex couples as not new to the children. In skills-based literacy work with younger children we used *One Dad Two Dads* as an example of a rhyming text, and took passages from other *No Outsiders* project books and removed the punctuation for punctuation skills practice. Older children looked at books intended for a younger audience, including some from the *No Outsiders* collection, and after considering their features, they used their learning to create stories for younger children.

Science

Children did work on stereotypes. They were given descriptions of scientific achievements or inventions and asked to draw what they thought the inventor or scientist looked like. Every child drew white non-disabled men. The teachers then showed them who the real scientists were and the scientists we presented reflected a cross-section of the community.

History

Under our school values of Respect and Unity, classes studied civil rights movements, including those for disability rights and gay rights. They examined changes in legislation such as the Disability Discrimination Act (1995), the Race Relations Amendment Act (2000) and the introduction of civil partnerships (2005).

Geography

Children designed buildings or environments and by this stage needed little prompting to consider the access needs of disabled people.

Personal, Social and Health Education (PSHE)

The need for specific work on homophobia, racism etc within PSHE diminished as the project continued. But the school did work on name-calling, returning constantly to the principle: 'We want everyone to feel welcome in our school'.

To Justin and Peter. I like your story. I enjoyed your story very much. Is Tango, Silo and Roy all right? Year 1 are painting and drawing pictures of Tango for you. We hope you like them.

Reading *King and King* to every class in the school *Kate*

> When I started to read the *King and King* book the first time, I never mentioned anything about the book – I didn't use it in any different way than I would have used any book in school. When I was reading it, the children themselves said, 'Does that mean they're gay?' and I said, 'Yes, it does' and one of the girls said, 'You can do it now [i.e. have a civil partnership] – it's legal. It used to be illegal but you can now,' and I said, 'That's right,' and that's all they said about it, and that was from them and not me. (Leanne)

I asked colleagues to read *King and King* to children from Reception (age 4-5) up to Year 6 (age 10-11). The younger children took the story at face value, a funny variation of the usual prince and princess stories. Any embarrassment was over kissing – this strange adult activity – and not the same sex storyline. But from Year 3 upwards, children showed increasing discomfort about the fact that it was about two men. The most extreme reaction came from the Year 4 class – 'That's disgusting!'

The Year 6 class, who had done a good deal of work in PSHE (Personal, Social and Health Education) and in the context of their history project on the Holocaust, recognised the theme early on – 'Oh Miss, this is a gay book isn't it?' They enjoyed the story, and then discussed the fact that there are gays and lesbians – and that's fine. We saw that each class looked to its leaders to set the tone. When a popular child received the book positively, the class generally followed. When the dominant boys in the Year 4 class responded with 'disgusting,' the others kept quiet.

I later found out from a parent that her son, who was in this class, had been taunted about being gay because he had said he wanted to live with his best friend when he grew up, as they liked doing the same things. The dominant boys backed down when challenged by the teacher on whether two men loving each other harmed others in any way, a challenge lightened by another child, who exclaimed,

> If boys did show affection to each other, they were instantly labelled as gay, but if girls did it, they were just being friendly and weren't seen immediately as being lesbian. (John)

'Yes, the princess would have felt hurt when he didn't choose her!' The discussion moved to the topic that not all relationships last, the children eager to share their experiences of parents and siblings splitting up with their partners. A big advantage of the primary classroom is that the session flagged up a number of issues which can be explored over the coming terms in several different curriculum areas.

> When I shared *King and King*, the Muslim parents were against the idea of their children being given the message that it was OK to be gay, because in their faith it was wrong. But they also said that they didn't want their children to be homophobic and call others names. (Sue K)

Making a film of *King and King* Leanne

King and King castles:

When I first introduced *King and King* and *King and King and Family* to my Year 1 class (age 5-6), the children turned our castle role play area into a King and King castle. In the book, there are lots of pictures on the castle walls, and the children went away and made pictures that tied in with the storybook. A lot of the boys who were – I know it sounds stereotypical – quite laddish, wanted to play football and tended to be a bit rough, started to do things like wearing pink dresses and wanting to be Princess Daisy, the name they'd given King and King's adopted baby, all the time. Until then, these boys hardly ever dressed up, and when they did it was to fight over the fireman's outfit and the policeman's outfit. Since making the *King and King* film, we've had a travel-agent's role play area where I'm sometimes the travel agent. I've noticed the children booking honeymoons, and last week two boys booked a honeymoon together.

Choosing roles for the *King and King* film:

When we were planning our *No Outsiders* week for the summer term, Miles said, 'Why don't you use your children's role play idea and get them to do their own play about *King and King*?' I asked whether we could possibly make a film instead, so the children won't feel self-conscious performing in front of everybody. At first, all the children wanted to be the Crown Kitty, and whenever I said, 'Who wants to be Prince Bertie?' they all just looked at me. Until I allocated that role they wouldn't volunteer for anything else. But as soon as I'd said, 'Right, B is Crown Kitty,' then it was hands up here, there and everywhere. The genders were completely mixed: girls wanting to be princes, boys wanting to be princesses. Earlier in the year, the boys had been more than happy to don a pink dress and spin around, but I wondered if that had changed now that they were a little older. I spread lots of costumes all over the classroom and said, 'You've got five minutes; go and choose your favourite outfit.' At least two of the boys chose very

Year 1 pupils making a film of *King and King*

feminine costumes of their own free will, and we cast two boys as the two princes who fall in love.

Kissing ...

We talked through the whole thing about the kiss, and about the picture of the two princes at the end of the book with a big heart in front of where their lips are touching. Every time I show it to them it they all burst out laughing. But that's because it's kissing, not because it's two men. I've said, 'What's funny about that? It's kissing!' And I talk about other (heterosexual) people kissing, but for them it's just, 'Urgh, no, it's kissing!' Their teacher for next year is getting married in the summer and she came in when we were doing *King and King* and talked to them about her forthcoming marriage. Miles came and talked about his civil partnership and showed photographs, and one of our Hindu members of staff told them about *her* wedding. So we were talking about lots of different weddings as well as *King and King*. But the children have a big thing about getting married: they find it hilarious, and that's to do with the kissing as well. The only thing they asked their new teacher was, 'Have you kissed your husband?' That's all. She said, 'Yes, I'm going to marry him, so I will kiss him.' It's just a fixation they have.

Telling the parents ...

I was very nervous about the parents' reactions to the two boys playing the princes. Although we send weekly newsletters out to parents, I knew they might not read them, and I wanted to be sure they did really know what their kids were doing. So when it came to the princes I rang the parents or caught them at home time and said, 'How do you feel about your son doing this? This is why he's been chosen.' And they said, 'Oh yeah, that's brilliant.' One of them said 'I don't know much about the story because he always loses his newsletter,' so I showed her the book and she said, 'Oh, I think that's really good that you are doing that, I am really pleased about it. I am really supportive of the work. I hadn't realised this was happening and I'm really excited he's going to play the part.' To be honest, that was not the reaction I was expecting from this parent. I was expecting, 'Oh, no, no, I don't want him to do that.' So I was pleasantly surprised and taken aback by the parents' reactions. I thought they were all just great.

When we showed the *King and King* film all the parents came and they all thought it was brilliant; they've said such positive things about it. So now we know we've got one whole class of children going through the school who have incredibly supportive parents, and I just love to think about the level of discussion they can go into when they are in Year 5 or 6. It will be lovely to watch the film with them when they are older, not just for nostalgia, but for them to say, 'What did we understand back then?'

> It's very difficult for a certain member of staff because she has deep set religious beliefs. It's not like she's homophobic in any way but personally she finds it difficult to get really heavily involved. But when she watched the film she said it was the best thing she'd seen since she's worked in this school - she's been here a long time. She said, 'You should take it to the press, it was brilliant.' And she told me, 'I was really worried it was all going to be about gay weddings but it's not about that, the children just take it at their level and a lot of the parents have said how much the children have enjoyed it.' (Leanne)

Working across the year groups
Nichola, Karen and Katie

Nichola, Karen and Katie work with different age groups in the same school. They have held a diversity week celebrating a wide range of different identities during the summer term, but have also embedded No Outsiders *project work across the whole year.*

Nichola: Teaching the Year 1 children (age 5-6) I felt I was laying the groundwork and that it wasn't hard at all, because they were so accepting. They celebrate any kind of difference, and they're really happy to let go of stereotypes that might have been part of their life. They are so accepting that 'Yeah, boys can do that and girls can do that,' and I feel proud that we've put that in place with them already and that it's so much a part of them, this acceptance.

We showed the *That's a Family* videos and read the books, and started from there to talk about relationships. They kept reminding each other about the connections: 'It's fine, remember *One Dad, Two Dad?*' I was reading *Oliver Button* is a Sissy today, and they were saying that it was lovely. They all enjoyed the story, but at the end where Oliver is saying, 'Will you let me be a ballet dancer?' three of the boys who are still coming to terms with the idea that someone might be different from them went, 'Ballet dancer? Boys?' But everyone else was saying, 'Yeah, of course he can be a ballet dancer.'

Karen: One of the boys in my Year 4 class (age 8-9) told the rest of the class about his brother being gay, just very matter of factly. I was delighted that the rest of the class just went, 'Can we move on?' It wasn't, 'Oooh'. And it's been good to be able to let colleagues know that when you've done something with a book the responses from the children are, 'Yeah, so what?' These are not the kind of response you would expect, and it makes other staff feel a little more comfortable about doing it themselves.

Nichola: I've made sure that support staff were in when we had the discussions. They felt cautious about it at first, and worried about saying the right thing, which is what we all felt. But having everyone being part of the discussion has been really good.

Katie: The first time we introduced one of the books, I read it to all of Year 6 (age 10-11) and had the other members of staff there. I read *King and King,* and when we came to the last page with the two princes kissing, one of the kids said, 'Oh, Mrs X, you are looking really red, what's the matter?' And I said, 'Well, actually sitting

The *Family Book* is used to explore different family patterns

here, reading to you, I am really worried: I'm not quite sure how you're going to react to this.' And the other two members of staff were relieved because they thought, 'If she's feeling that, then it's alright for us to feel that way.' And I think me telling the kids that I was slightly worried about how they would react made them feel better about coming out and saying how they felt.

Nichola: I put some of the books into my literacy plan, because most of them are rich material for literacy teaching. We did something on fairy tales and started with the *Paper Bag Princess* as an alternative fairy tale, then moved on to *King and King*. I typed up a script version of it and we acted it out. I changed my role-play area into a castle and the children were acting it

out in there. I often had boys dressing up as princesses and the girls as knights anyway, so it was nice to give them more opportunity than usual to do that.

Karen: We didn't deliberately use it as part of our literacy, but we read *King and King* and the kids loved it. So I said, 'Oh, there's another one – it's *King and King and Family*' – and read it the next day. We'd been looking at sentence structure and word choice, and they commented that the sentence structure wasn't very good and suggested different words they would have chosen and said they might have done a better job. So they treated it as a literacy book rather than an issue book or anything like that. They really didn't like *King and King and Family*, as they thought it wasn't well written. I think this is interesting in light of our long discussion about the book.

Nichola: In terms of drip-feeding in the wider area of diversity, we've always spent a lot of time saying, 'It doesn't matter what you look like, we are the same on the inside.' I think the message has changed over time into, 'It doesn't matter what you look like on the outside or the inside', and that's good.

From a tentative start to a full-scale opera
John

As a non-class-based deputy head, I had the opportunity to carry out project work in different classes. I began by reading the books myself and thinking about which I could use that would cause the least uproar from the parents. The school I work in is approximately 70 percent African-Caribbean; other children are from Asian, Mediterranean and Eastern European families. The great majority of the children identify as Christian with the next major religious group being Muslim.

I dismissed *King and King*, perhaps too hastily, as I felt uncomfortable with the storyline. At the time I wondered, 'Will I be able to counter any negative reactions to the book without becoming too emotionally involved?' The answer to both these questions is now a resounding YES: I'm fine with it and have read it to groups without any fear. But I think I felt exposed as a gay man at the early stage of the project.

I tried to ease myself and the kids into the work I proposed to do by reading *The Sissy Duckling* to Year 5 (age 9-10). I copped out by asking them to evaluate the book's suitability for Key Stage 1 (age 5-7) and Key Stage 2 (age 7-11). This shifted the focus away from what the story was actually about, helping me to avoid any potentially embarrassing questions about the issues in the book. The reactions to the story were very positive. No one focused on the 'sissy' element of the book even though I explained the word to the children as 'boys not behaving in ways that people think boys should be like'. Then one boy tried calling another sissy: the class, as one, stopped work and collectively took a breath. As one, they rounded on the boy and told him, 'It's not acceptable to use that word. Why do you think John just read that story?' I didn't need to say a thing – relief and a huge sense of pride and achievement!

We had a visit by a gay black student teacher, who read *And Tango Makes Three* with one of the boys. The student said how pleasantly surprised he was that such a book had been written that he was and even more surprised by the child's lack of reaction to the story. The pupil had said,

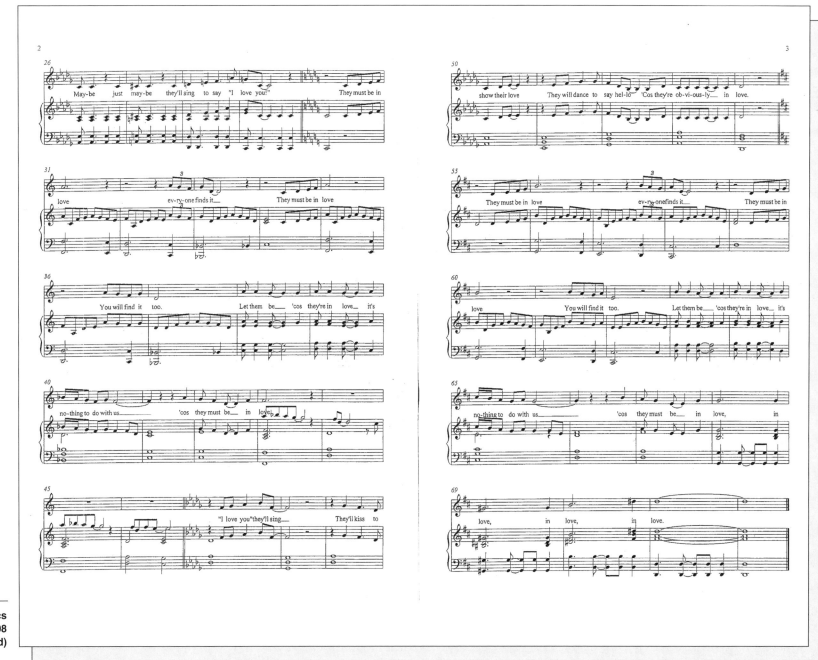

'Oh, those penguins must be gay'; the student replied, 'Yes' and that was it. I continued to read the books with different year groups, including using them for two years to boost literacy skills with groups of high ability children in Year 6.

We looked for books the pupils could use to write a libretto for an opera, for which I would compose the music. They came up with the idea of combining *And Tango Makes Three* and *Oliver Button is a Sissy* to make a kind of gay version of Happy Feet. The next year's group decided to narrow the focus for the opera down to the story of *Tango*. They took to it readily and produced some thoughtful and interesting lyrics. The absence of any negative reaction to the story has surprised and delighted me. When I remarked that Roy and Silo were gay but that the g-word hadn't been mentioned in the book at all, one boy said that it might have put people off buying the book, remarking that 'Some people still have a problem with that these days'!

The reactions of the children to some of the books ranged from indifference to complete negativity. One boy kept saying, 'No; this is wrong; The Bible says it's wrong', to which I replied, 'Is this the same Bible that says, 'Love thy neighbour'?' Another boy disclosed to the group that his uncle is gay. There was no reaction to this statement and the boy was not ridiculed afterwards or put down in any way. Another victory!

The opera has now been performed several times in school, as well as at a borough-wide LGBT History Month event, with yet another group of children taking the parts of the children who have gone on to secondary school.

I've still to read more books to the rest of the school. I don't want it to be seen as just my work because I'm the only gay teacher – I want the others to include the books in their classroom work and discuss them. I intend planning work for every class to do based on the books. I've created a Diversity display as an inroad, albeit very small, into doing something for LGBT History Month (every February). I've collected together books about the family from the project and from the school library. I wrote labels about how we celebrate differences at our school and how we value everyone, and put up the Real Families Rock poster created by *Out For Our Children*.

But I'm essentially unhappy about this, as the display is tucked away in an alcove where only a small section of the school community will see it. I feel that as we make such a big thing about Black History Month, we should do the same here. Perhaps we're not as inclusive a school as we make out!

No Outsiders has helped me to re-examine issues around my own sexual orientation. Why, for instance, did I choose to read *Hello, Sailor* – which is not one of the project books, but used by several teachers in the project – to Year 2 and not Year 5? Was I so terrified of answering awkward questions? Why have I chosen not to include *We Do* in the books I have used with the children? Will I grow to like *King and King*? Why don't I like it?

I am also ready to come out to the pupils and their parents. When will the school be ready? And will I get the support I deserve?

Laura: I'm really concerned that I find myself latching on to knowable safe images of gay daddies and lesbian mummies or at least gay and lesbian couples falling in love. I guess I'm partly led to this safe, middle of the road place by the project books, which inscribe these notions of romantic, monogamous relationships – albeit with gay people or penguins rather than straight ones.

Andrew: I just like the fact that we are talking about gay penguins. I don't think we need to get beyond that at this stage. We are in the early stages of this nationally, this sort of thinking. The fact that we've got gay penguins is fantastic; why do we need to worry about what's next? We need to get schools to talk about gay penguins because at the moment most schools aren't doing anything.

Funky Families: Telling All!
Sue E

Sue's work was embedded all through her school's involvement in the project, but in the summer term of each of the two years, she held a festival of celebration. The first lasted a week and the second a fortnight. Here she talks about the personal input she and her colleagues made to the Funky Families Fortnight, and the ways in which the children responded.

There was dawning realisation among the staff about how their families differed, and how different the family groups in the school were too. For example, we were excited that Father's Day fell on the first weekend of our fortnight and thought: Great – we can do Father's Day cards!

Then we realised that in fact not all the children had dads and some had step dads. The fathers of no fewer than four children had committed suicide, several fathers had died and some were in the middle of splitting up and divorce. We realised that the Father's Day thing was another myth.

So that changed our view on how to treat Father's Day cards in the school.

We decided that the teachers would rotate around the classes and every teacher would tell their own family story to the children. My opportunity came in assembly. I drew a family tree of my grandparents, showing that one had been a teacher, because I thought that would interest the children, and that another had lied about his age and joined the army. Another was in a wheelchair, so that brought in disability and we talked about that – and she was married to a chap who had a glass eye. Then I added my mother and father to the family tree, plus a picture of me and my sister, and I said how jealous I had been of my sister.

I went on to say I had a fairytale wedding, best day of my life and all that, and had three gorgeous children. Then I talked about the time when my husband fell in love with another woman: I had never shared anything so personal ever ever ever, you know, with children. But I thought I really needed to talk about it. This was with

the whole school and staff, you know, and I said, 'He fell in love with another woman and left me! And I was very, very sad.' And they all went, 'Ooooh'. I carried on, saying it's a good family, it's me and my three children, we work as a team and we've really good times together and we'd adjusted, our family had changed but it is still great. And how our friends were very important to us as well.

> Children come from all sorts of different family backgrounds and have all kinds of different experiences that don't fit into the nice little neat box, and you don't want any child to think, 'Nobody would understand my family' (Teacher, North East)

> Well, it doesn't matter if you've got two mams, or just a mam with no dad, if you've got two dads or just one dad - it doesn't matter – you're just still a family.
> (Year 3 pupil, North East)

I felt utterly exhausted from having shared this intensely personal story with my school but asked, 'Right, are there any questions?' And all these hands went up, as they do, and it was one of those *No Outsiders* moments, thinking, 'What are they going to ask me?' And do you know what? They wanted to know about my grandfather's glass eye! That was all they asked me about, you know, why was he blind etc! When I asked, 'Are there any other questions?' another child wanted to know why my grandfather had lied about his age to go into the army, and I saw that

So you've got marriage, yes, which is an option; you've got people who are single; or you've got people who've had civil partnerships; you've got people who just live together. I would like to have the words changed from 'How do we celebrate marriage' to maybe 'How do we celebrate commitment'. (Jon)

the teachers were laughing. I said, 'I poured my heart out here and all they want to know about is glass eyes!'

There were two brothers in school at that time who were in the process of being adopted. So we asked Matthew, the vicar, to come in and talk about being adopted, because he's adopted too. When he talked to the class with the older of these two boys in it, the child said for the first time, 'I am adopted'. Matthew told the class how Jesus was adopted by Joseph, then asked the boy, 'Do you realise that you, me and Jesus all have something in common? We're all adopted. Isn't that special?'

We had a sculptor in who'd made a lovely wooden sculpture of a family. It was of a baby being held above the head of a child standing on the shoulders of another child, standing on the shoulders of a woman standing on the shoulders of a man. And at one point he turned it upside down so it looked as though the family was sort of

pressing down on top of the baby and said, 'It wouldn't work like that, would it?' Knowing we had children in the school who were young carers, I joined in, asking the class while the sculpture was upside down, 'Don't say anything but just put your hand up if you've ever felt like this baby.' And quite a few of them put their hands up. Again, it was fine for them to acknowledge that they do sometimes feel that they are carrying the weight of their family.

Another time, the mother of one child came to talk to the children about being a foster-parent, and she also told the children that she was a lesbian.

She brought a family book with her parents' pictures of when she was a baby, then showed a picture of her family with her three children from when she was married to her husband. Then she showed a picture of herself with her lesbian partner on the sofa and said, 'Here we all are having a cuddle on the sofa, because we believe cuddles are important. Don't you agree?' And they all agreed. Two governors were still thinking all the time that we had this over-emphasis on lesbian and gay people, which I might have accepted if every single member of staff had not given their family story and also anybody who came into the school.

lesbian foster-mother talks about what makes a family

Coming out at Art Club
Kate

I have been out to staff and governors for a while now – but not out to parents I did not know well or to the children. During a recent art club session I was leading as part of a Holocaust Memorial project with a Year 6 class (age 10-11; not my own class) I came out as a lesbian. It was a very important moment for me, and although I had not been hidden, I hadn't felt I could come out before. I have heard children saying, literally behind my back, that their older brother or sister who was no longer at the school has told them I'm a lesbian, but I had chosen to avoid the situation by 'not hearing' such comments. Coming out had to be something that happened in an appropriate context, and this was exactly right. I had thought before the session that I might say I was gay, but I wasn't quite sure I would. I used to teach this class, so felt at ease with them and they with me. Not teaching them now – except in art club – made it easier.

The session (see the plan in Chapter 7) was based around the labels used by Nazis to identify various groups of people they deemed 'unacceptable', plus other labels and words – racist terms, informative labels (e.g. the disabled wheelchair symbol), symbols adopted by groups themselves (rainbow flag, Christian fish, Muslim crescent moon etc). Children sorted the labels into the categories 'good' and 'bad' – provoking much discussion in groups, particularly around the term 'gay'. One boy described gay as 'minging' and 'disgusting'- a boy who has enjoyed 'girlish' things throughout his time at school, but is now under pressure, particularly from his father, to play with the boys and do more 'boyish' activities.

The session went on to look at the Nazis' views and then what the children thought the views were in today's society and who the 'outsiders' are now. I ran the session with the Year 6 teacher, a Muslim, and led up to coming out by discussing how she might feel when 'Muslim' and 'Paki' were used as terms of abuse. Then I picked up the pink triangle and said, 'I'm gay. Is that minging?' The children's reaction made me feel very accepted and supported. Even the boy who had described gay as 'minging' wanted to be sure I knew that he didn't think *I* was minging – and it was liberating for him to say that people called him gay. In the flood of ensuing comments, children talked about gay members of their family, their parents and gay friends.

I'm sure word about me spread through the school, but I have had no comeback, nor has any been reported by staff. I did, however, hear from a couple of the parents of children who attended the session. They described their children as 'buzzing' when they came out of it. One parent, who had her daughter while in a lesbian relationship, and now lives with the father, said it had prompted a very meaningful conversation between her and her daughter about sexuality and relationships. I too was buzzing with what had happened – this felt like one of the most important sessions I've ever been in, one in which real discussion makes a difference to people's lives.

New year failure
A child asked me if I was married. What a golden opportunity to come out to a member of my class! But no, I just didn't feel I had the emotional energy so told her I wasn't married but did have a partner. Nuff said. (Kate)

New year success:
Science lesson on magnets: children experimenting and feeling the push of magnets and realising for the first time that they repel as well as attract. Recording in cartoon form so the children would remember. One child commented – 'Like how boys are attracted to girls then?' Response, 'Yes, and how also boys can be attracted to boys and girls can be attracted to girls' Response from children? Slightly along the 'yuk' factor scale. More to do with attraction generally, I think, than specifically to same sex. But will it help them remember the science! (Kate)

From abuse to congratulations
Miles

On the last day of the Christmas term, I went out to talk to some boys who had shouted through the school fence at a colleague. As I walked out one child shouted at me: 'You fucking gay bastard, we know you shag the kids'. It wasn't the best last afternoon before Christmas! As a child I would have kept quiet and worried that others would think badly of me for being bullied. But as an adult the difference was that I discussed it with colleagues, confident that they would be horrified and supportive. A year later, as one of the boys involved in that incident was helping take down cards in my office, including cards to myself and my partner, he asked, 'How was your civil partnership?'

Just before our civil partnership ceremony, I read *King and King* in a Year 5 and 6 assembly (age 9 -11) and told the children that I had a similar situation, as I and my male partner were marrying at half term. The children were very still. At circle-time with Year 6 children, I said that I realised they would have different reactions to my news, but it turned out that most of the class already knew I was gay. We talked about the incident the previous Christmas and how I had felt about the name calling. I asked whether they felt they had ever been called names because other children thought they were different and everyone said they had. I returned to the subject of my sexuality and invited comments. Some children were keen to jump in, with comments like, 'You should be able to live your life how you want', 'I think it's fine' and, 'You should be able to choose what you want to do'. I told them it was likely that someone they knew at school would grow up to be gay and this made a few of them glance at each other – reassuring each other, I think, that it wasn't them. I asked if this would make them feel differently about one another, and they claimed not. One child said they didn't think any differently about me so it would be the same if it was one of their friends. I said that I hoped this was the case.

At lunchtime many of the children congratulated me and wished me well. At the end of the day a group of girls came to my room with cards they had made for me and my partner. A parent and her three children also brought in a card and a bottle of wine, saying, 'We're so pleased and wanted you to know how great we think it is'. My Deputy informed me that the one boy still in school who had been involved in the 'fence' incident the previous Christmas had told her he was going to make me a good luck card.

My whole attitude about talking about myself has changed and I feel confident about my sexuality in terms of my work. I've learned something really important from this: that as an authority figure in the school who happens to be gay, I have a responsibility to talk about it because that can change people's attitudes. Sometimes I think, 'Oh, I don't want to make a fuss. I want to be just normal', but that's not just going to happen overnight. It's only by sticking your neck out that it becomes normalised for people. Sometimes you have to take a step into the unknown darkness to seek out support.

Why is your wife not cooking?

Hello all, thought I would email everybody to say thank you for the *No Outsiders* project. This is what happened on Thursday afternoon. I am in my new school now, so all that I have learned from the project is proving useful and is a reason that the project should be carried on despite bad press.

We were dancing in PE about 'Ourselves'. We each had to think of three things that represented us at home, at school and out of home/school. Whilst miming my action for home (which wasn't anything gay at all – despite what the *Daily Mail* might think!) I pretended to beat a cake mixture. A 6 year-old girl asked me in a big loud voice, 'Why is your wife not cooking?'

Before I had chance to reply, a boy, also aged 6 and with a massive, cute smile, said matter of factly, 'Because he's gay, silly!' When the little girl didn't respond, he said, 'You know, gay, when two men love each other. He lives with a man!' Then he said, 'You *are* gay, aren't you?' To which I replied (half-stunned), 'Yes!' The boy then proceeded to tell other children who were hearing range about me being gay. I didn't have the heart to tell him to stop, although he was rather excited about letting others know. I just thought, 'Well I'm not going to lie . . .'

Before the project, I would never have been able to say yes to the boy's question because I wouldn't have had the confidence. The subject of being gay wouldn't have been on my list of priorities to talk about with the kids but, hey, it made me feel good. Now I don't have to go out of my way not to mention my partner etc. And it caused some laughter when I retold my 'outing' by a 6 year old to my Teaching Assistants next morning. (Jon)

Working with primary trainee teachers
Katherine

During the second year of the project, Katherine moved from a primary school to a lecturing post at a teacher training institution. Here she describes how she took her project work into primary teacher training.

As part of the Primary English programme for the Postgraduate Certificate in Education (PGCE) students, the English team planned a session on gender-based texts and current issues, and I took this opportunity to lead a *No Outsiders* session with each group of students (see Chapter 7 for related planning). I felt quite nervous about what the reaction would be, as I knew this cohort could be very vocal, but they really engaged with the session. They felt that this is a real issue that trainees have to deal with in school, for which they receive little training.

I started each of the sessions by encouraging the students to agree that everyone should feel free to express their views and that no-one would be judged for their opinions or feelings. I think this was invaluable as it gave freedom to some students to say that they didn't feel comfortable with either the subject matter or some of the books, and that they didn't feel able to use them in schools with the children. This led to some interesting debate among the students.

It was immensely interesting and humbling to bear witness to these discussions. The project books themselves provoked the most discussion. Each student identified their favourite and how they thought they might use them in class. They were keen to hear about my own experiences with the project in my school and about other project schools across the country. One student actually cried when she saw the photo in *We Do* of the first female couple to get married in San Francisco – an older couple who had been together for many years. She said all children should be able to see love like that. This provoked much discussion about how the book caused upset in some of the project schools.

> Thousands upon thousands of primary school age children have openly lesbian and gay family members ... How better to explain these relationships to children than through storytelling and celebration? (Letter to The *Observer*)

In the summer term, we were able to bring in Dean, the performance poet who had worked with children in some of the project schools, to work with another group of primary trainee teachers in their penultimate year of training.

The discussions held after each of the sessions showed just how engaged the students were, and reflected their enthusiasm and drive to work with the project when they were on teaching placement and ultimately when they have their own classes. Many of the students emailed to say how valuable the session had been. One student wrote, 'Just wanted to say a huge thank you for such an amazing workshop on Thursday! It was probably the best thing we have done during the whole three years!' And another: 'I know I speak for a lot of us when I say it was one of the most useful, interactive and enjoyable workshops I have been to. Dean was inspiring and I hope the project goes far.'

After an event at which Mark Jennett, the project's diversity trainer, and Jay Stewart of *Gendered Intelligence* both spoke, I wrote:

> The day was a huge success and the students (and some staff) learnt a great deal from it. The number of students

Trainee teachers work with Dean on notions of community

43

who have asked how they can get involved with the project in the future is astonishing! Many students have since sought me out to ask if there would be an opportunity for it to be embedded in the BEd (Bachelor of Education) course as they think it is so central to everything we do as teachers.

In my experience in both school and in college, what has really mattered is the interest or support of other people: not just people in management, but also colleagues and students. There is strength in numbers, and whenever we managed to get lots of like-minded people together, they seemed to give the project power. Supportive and understanding parents made a massive difference to me in school, as it gave me permission for the work I was doing and made it seem OK when perhaps the other members of the school weren't so keen.

This belief that came from others has really supported me, both as a project teacher in school and in my new role in teacher education. It has been an honour to have the opportunity to work on such a ground-breaking project with such a powerful message and to share this message with so many people. I especially value the opportunity to share the work with the students, as I feel that they will take the message further and disseminate it in all the schools they work in in future. And what also really makes a difference is the unwavering belief that what you are doing is right and important, despite the misrepresentations in the media. This belief is made possible by working alongside such a supportive, passionate and inspiring project team.

For me the barriers to moving forward at school were:

- the head teacher not showing as much interest and support as she might have

- the governing body reacting to the project in an automatically negative way without fully considering the project aims

- the scaremongering media

It's not good to feel that you are working alone, and where other staff think what you are doing is odd or wrong and shouldn't be for children's ears.

At university level, it seems that mentioning the word 'homophobia' makes some lecturers fearful, but I feel this is due less to prejudice than to lack of understanding about how to teach the students how to cope with it in the primary classroom when they themselves have never had to tackle it.

I have learned so much from the project, not just about how to challenge homophobia in the classroom but about myself, too. I feel really dedicated to the project and the team of people I have grown to know and respect, and that a huge amount has been achieved in the space of a couple of years. I am proud to be a member of this team.

> I am so, so, so, so, so excited and had to email you to share my excitement! I had a module meeting today to organise our 'current issues' module for next term and I have managed to get my one hour *No Outsiders* workshop to a WHOLE ENTIRE DAY with 180 students! (Katherine)

Chapter 4

Reflections

Relationships are key
David

When I first became involved in the project I didn't recognise that relationships are crucial in collaborative action research projects, not just the icing on the cake. That the relationship is the data and vice versa. Reflecting now on my work as a research assistant for the project, what did I learn from working with seven teachers in five schools? Or rather, what did they teach me and how?

My reflections fall into three overlapping sections: what they taught me about primary schools, what they taught me about human nature and what they taught me about working on an 'edgy' project. To state the obvious, I learnt how much primary schools differ: although the schools had all opted into *No Outsiders*, and so presumably shared some underlying commitment to diversity and inclusion, there were clear differences between even two schools which were in walking distance of each other.

I'm not talking about differences which are quantifiable or to do with league tables but of feel, atmosphere or perhaps culture. One very modern school in which everything looked good *felt* a little impersonal; one rather run-down looking school *felt* like a comfy armchair; one school in a picture postcard village was more diverse and radical than its mellow stones suggested. The only conclusion might be that primary schools are small communities which take on their own culture in a way which is relatively independent of central control, and depends rather on the character and history of individuals and locations.

The teachers I worked with reminded me similarly of the diversity of human nature.

Those in leadership roles exercised authority by force of personality and caring competence, showing the ability to move easily in our conversations between this public leadership role and something more personal. Classroom teachers were highly committed to the project's principles even when support from their school leadership was hazy or doubtful. Together, we took a journey of personal and professional discovery in which the relationships between us were key.

In the second year, the challenges and risks of the project became more apparent. In two of the schools I worked with, opposition to education towards sexualities equality was based on a particular faith position. In a third, the head teacher, whose stance towards the project had always been lukewarm, used some negative publicity that arose from the first two schools as an excuse to suspend activities. In a fourth school, a minor example of inappropriate language threatened to blow up out of proportion, whereas the fifth school seemed relatively unaffected by their own and others' emerging challenges, after spending many early months dealing with difficulties.

As a result, almost none of the teacher-researchers remained unaffected or escaped negative consequences, whether professional or personal or both. But nowhere in this process was their commitment to the underlying work of inclusion compromised. If we as a university research team felt occasionally exposed, frustrated, irritated, we were nonetheless not on the front line as the teachers were daily. It is not for me to evaluate their response to these challenges, but I observed them growing in this process, sometimes painfully, both personally and professionally. And so did I.

> I know that I will never lose sight of the enormous impact the No Outsiders project has had on my professional and personal life, on my colleagues, pupils and families. This has been one of the best experiences of my life - it has had huge ups and downs. It has been emotional and life changing. I am overwhelmingly pleased to have been part of it. (Miles)

Being human
Elizabeth B

Working on the project as a university-based research assistant alongside teacher-researchers, activists and other university researchers has been inspirational. These talented and committed people have achieved so much, often against what seemed like overwhelming odds. Their work has impacted on other teachers, schools and local authorities, many of whom are taking the project's work forward in their own contexts.

The actual doing of the project was in many ways different from what I'd expected, particularly in relation to the way in which it has allowed for, or even forced, project members to be human and not impartial researchers or observers. I knew this might be a difficult project for the teachers working at the frontline in their schools. I imagined there would be times when they would feel uncertainty or frustration – for instance, I'd always anticipated that others would question what they were doing and perhaps put barriers in their way. But I didn't anticipate the complex ways in which the project

work interacted with the teachers' personal identities, lives and relationships and how the work might challenge and change their views and understandings of equalities and education. I have been hugely privileged to witness what went on.

The doing of the project, and the differences between this and my original expectations, has affected me too. In particular, it has challenged my perception that working on a large project alongside other people, and initiated by other people, would necessarily be done in a distanced way. For instance, I found that the project website, which had a private area for project members, became a place where we met as people and brought along our own lives, experiences and opinions. A discussion of our own sexual identities became central to the work we were doing. This discussion and others like it helped team members to become friends and allies in a context where friends and allies sometimes seemed to be in short supply.

> Another beautiful and unexpected by-product of the project is the new friendships I've formed with colleagues in the project team and with schools and other organisations where I've delivered training. I really value these new relationships for their emotional and practical support and hope they continue.
> (John)

This personal aspect of the project also brought its discomforts. Even though the website offered us a potentially safe space, most of us nevertheless took risks when we exposed our discomforts to each other. Our differences were made clear too and as a result I often found myself thinking hard about the 'best' way to do or think about things – although often, in the end, there wasn't a best way. One of the great findings of this project is that people are all different, they think differently, and they take many different approaches to challenging heteronormativity and homophobia.

The discussions often challenged implicit norms relating to sexuality, gender, education, and the relationships between adults and children that we reinforce. For example, I was guilty of sexualising gay and lesbian people, in that I felt there was a reason for people to object to the project's aims – even if I didn't agree with it myself.

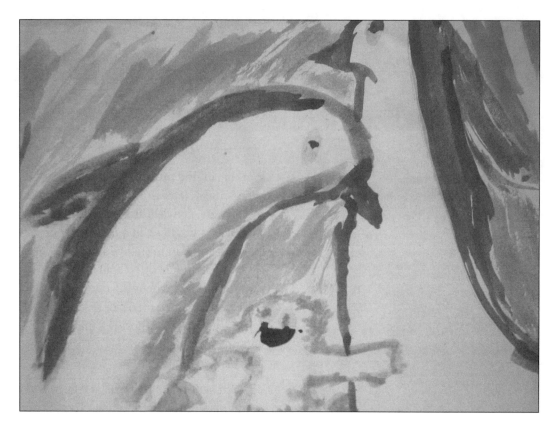

Implicitly, I was buying into the view that the project involved teaching children about gay sex, even though I actually knew it did nothing of the sort. However, as I questioned these and other assumptions during the course of the project, I learnt to view our aims in terms of human rights.

Year 4 pupil's painting based on *And Tango Makes Three*

> I still have this thing in my head that you can tell all the LGBT people because they look different. But then I'm thinking no, actually, that person you're taking to be an absolutely straight guy, or an absolutely straight woman, is as likely to be gay as anybody else. And that's so refreshing.
> (Elizabeth A)

Memories and reflections
Jon

Knowing I was gay

I don't know whether I knew I was gay when I was at primary school. I knew I was different. I never had many friends so there was that kind of being on your own anyway, so I was always different that way as well. Being in the shadow of a twin sister doesn't help either. But I remember fancying boys when I was four, but I didn't know whether it was fancying, or just, I don't know, that they were nice. But I knew, probably when I got to secondary school and people started telling me that I was.

Past life ...

Walking home from a friend´s place with my ex-partner one night, we were beaten up. You know, we were just a couple of blokes walking down the street and, well, there were five of them behind us, and one shouted out, 'Oy, are you gay?' So we just

> Gay and lesbian and bisexual people shouldn't be very afraid to say it (Year 5 pupil, London)

carried on walking, and they just beat us up for the hell of it. But why were we beaten up? I mean we'll never know the answer to that really. The police knew it was a homophobic assault, but they kind of said, 'Well, why were you walking home at that time of night?'

Announcing our civil partnership in the school newsletter

Our civil partnership was announced in the newsletter, but they didn't give my partner's name. They just said, 'Congratulations to Jon and his partner'. So I don't know whether it's kind of ambiguous: if you don't know what a civil partnership is, it just sounds as though you could just be straight. But it was good to have the announcement all the same. I asked for it to be afterwards, though. Normally, if there are weddings in school, they get announced beforehand, but this was a sort of insurance, really. I didn't want anybody spoiling the best day that's going to happen to us.

Talking about family diversity

I did a half hour citizenship enrichment assembly with the Key Stage 1 classes (age 5-7) and we talked about families and their roles and relationships. We did a big introduction to what families are and what families do. We talked about the characteristics of families, that they love each other, do different things together, play together and so on. I had lots of pictures of different families, so we talked about the wheelchairs, the dog, the single parents – and then we had the two mums. In our training, Mark had suggested saying, 'Oh yeah, lucky enough to have two mums,' so I said that. There was no comment on the two mums, nothing. It was just accepted as actually yeah, that is a family. And then the only other comment that we got at the end was where there was a picture of a large family, with a mum at the front and a dad in the middle, and other adults as well, but one little boy at the front of the hall said, 'Wow, two dads'. That was a nice surprise because it wasn't actually two dads but it could have been. So I said, 'Oh yeah, if that's what you think'. But there's also a little boy in Year 1 who does have two mums, and when they went back to class, I know the teacher did a discussion on that.

> We are going to set up a small display and put up photos of children and a person they love. It doesn't matter who you love, it doesn't matter what your family looks like. You can love who you want. As part of the display my teaching assistant will have a photo of her and her husband, and I will put a picture up of me and my partner. (Jon)

Two years in
Judy

Judy reflects on her experiences at the end of the second year of the project.

I've done a series of Key Stage 1 assemblies (age 5-7) using a different episode of the *That's a Family* DVD each week. This was fantastic, absolutely fantastic, because it was just showing the diversity of families, and the children are more than happy to talk about their family and what their experiences are. So by the time you get to something like single sex families they are completely at ease with all sorts of families and they say there are two men together or two women together and that's OK.

The only children who picked up on it negatively were a few of the eldest in Key Stage 1, and it struck me that their families' opinions were coming through the children: 'My father says that if two blokes are together it's not right.' But I always made a point of having the parent liaison worker in there as well, so that if parents pick up on the fact that the children are using the words gay and lesbian, she would be able to put this in context for them.

I did the story *If I had 100 Mummies* and a girl who has two mummies put her hand up and said, 'Well, I've got two mummies.'

And we framed it that she is the luckiest one to have two mummies, because we'd all like 100 kisses at bedtime and 100 ice creams if we went out to play. One of her mums came in and told the class teacher how pleased she was. I think it was refreshing for mum that her situation was being framed as a norm. The class teacher told her that it wasn't because her child had come to the school that we were addressing these issues; the project was already in place, and that really reassured her.

A teaching assistant came to me the other day and said, 'Oh, a child has just been called a lesbian by another. What shall I do?' And I said, 'What do you think?' and she said, 'Well, I will go and get a book.' It was during the maths lesson and she got the book and read it to the child who'd used 'gay' as an insult and said, 'Now what do you understand by the word gay?' But the ethos of the school is if somebody came up in maths and said, 'I haven't had any breakfast,' then they'd be taken out and given a biscuit. So it wasn't the fact that it was a gay issue, it would have been dealt with at once if it had been anything at all.

**Dean Atta, a performance p[...]
who worked with pupils and [...]
trainee teachers in the proje[...]
(www.myspace.com/deanat[...]**

Including sexualities equality as a core Christian value
Sue E

Sue is the head teacher of a small Church of England village school. Here she describes how her school took on sexualities equality as a core inclusion value and a fundamental tenet of its overall Christian ethos.

The seeds were sown for me to join the *No Outsiders* project as I sat in a cathedral amongst a congregation made up of leaders from church schools, listening to an address by Rowan Williams, Archbishop of Canterbury. The address was inspiring, but it was the Archbishop's response to a question about the inequalities endured by LGBT people which stayed with me. His reply was uncharacteristically vague and non-committal, yet he clearly recognised the anguish they suffered. Later that day I was checking my emails and found an invitation for schools in my region to join the *No Outsiders* project, named after a quote by Archbishop Desmond Tutu.

Initially I thought, 'But we are a really small primary school, it's not really an issue here'. We do have members of the school community who are gay, and we have children who have gay parents and people in the wider community who are gay too, but I didn't really feel in my heart that it was an issue and I wasn't sure what use I'd be. In addition, the school had been failed by Ofsted at its inspection and all my energy needed to be focused on improving standards.

But actually sexualities equality has become important precisely *because* we're a small village, predominantly white and middle class, and I've started to understand that the whole gay thing is hidden. There is nobody yet saying, 'I am the only gay in the village' and there is certainly more than one who is![1]

I signed our school up for the *No Outsiders* project because it is a church school that takes the Christian ethos very seriously. A few months earlier the staff had defined the core values of the school, firmly setting them within the Christian foundation of the school. One of our core values was inclusion. As we explored these values over time I saw an opportunity to introduce sexualities equality within the context of inclusion.

[1] 'I'm the only gay in the village' is the popular catch phrase of a gay character in the comedy series *Little Britain*, a UK series aimed at an adult audience. For an analysis of Andy's response to a child's use of this phrase in a primary school context, see *Interrogating Heteronormativity* (Trentham, 2009), chapter 1.

Jesus is teaching love thy neighbour, full stop. And so which neighbours do we not love, which neighbours do we cross off the list? Do we cross off the homeless, do we cross off homosexuals, do we cross off people we don't like, and is that a Christian way to be? He didn't say love which neighbours, he said love them all. (Jo, reporting on a sermon given by the local curate).

I announced at a staff meeting that I had signed up the school for the *No Outsiders* project. Staff appeared a little sceptical at first; there was some giggling, some awkward moments. We looked at some of the children's literature provided by the project, and while some of the books went into classrooms, they seemed to disappear into book corners rather than be used explicitly for classroom teaching. I didn't know at first how to breathe life into the work.

I included in my written report to governors a matter of fact statement that we had joined the project, explaining that it was a natural extension of our work on inclusion. Coincidentally, we had also decided to work for the Inclusion Quality

'I love you' emotion machine: part of a drama workshop presentation. Year 5 and 6 pupils

Mark (IQM), a nationally-recognised award which requires schools to develop and implement a rigorous action plan to ensure good inclusive practice throughout all aspects of the school's life. It was a powerful move to link our participation in the *No Outsiders* project explicitly to our work toward achieving the IQM, because Ofsted recognises the IQM and we were very eager to receive a good Ofsted report. Three governors' meetings went by with the *No Outsiders* project as an item on the agenda before a governor asked a question about it. I began to sense that they, like the staff, felt insecure about how to talk about the project in a meaningful way.

Mark Jennett's diversity training seemed to help. All the governors and staff were invited, although only a few governors came. Giving people the words and understandings and letting them have open discussions proved pivotal in moving the project forward. Everyone who attended talked about it afterwards in a way that suggested a kind of openness about not knowing, and a beginning to know. We also incorporated the Archbishop Tutu quote that inspired *No Outsiders* directly into our schools' inclusion policy.

By the summer term, it was relatively easy for us to theme our traditional arts week as a *No Outsiders* week and focus on areas of inclusion. I was delighted that the idea did not come from me: I was seeing staff taking ownership of the initiative. What surprised and pleased me most about the week was the way in which some teachers – not all – took some of the project books and worked with them without prompting. An infant class teacher fashioned a whole literacy topic around *King and King* and *King and King and Family*; another teacher analysed *The Harvey Milk Story* in terms of its autobiographical features. We had four days of input from a professional drama company, who also worked with some of the project books.

We constructed a *No Outsiders* banner with a rainbow background, and on the last day of the arts week children processed with this banner to the local village church, where they performed presentations for parents and other community members. At the end of the ceremony, the local vicar announced, 'Jesus was really into *No Outsiders* as well. He always went to look for the people who were on the edge.'

I have always been a strong believer in justice, and I began to see that I had to do some challenging, and that my powerful role as head teacher gave me a kind of mandate to do so. I thought of the little I could do as a kind of 'stirring'. At first I understood this to mean stirring things up, being a bit of a trouble-maker. Now, as I reflect on this metaphor, I like the double meaning of the word: stirring as an awakening, and stirring that in. The project

> We have been awarded the Inclusion Quality Mark and the assessors really liked the project and the books, so I feel the work of *No Outsiders* was very much affirmed by that. (Sue E)

has forced a stirring within people. This suggests something very small, a small still voice which has the potential to become something louder and greater, but has equal potential to fade away altogether, leaving not even an uneasy silence. I hope people can be encouraged to follow this stirring on to further more powerful equality work.

Impossible boy-girls in the numeracy lesson: putting poststructuralist theory into practice
Laura

During my involvement in the *No Outsiders* project, I feel I have re-engaged with the poststructuralist tools I used as an English undergraduate to help me to understand the ways in which meanings about gender and sexuality are created in my classroom. Engaging with theory whilst working as a full time teacher of a Year 3 class provides me with different ways of understanding the children I teach and gives me a means by which to see the discourses circulating in my classroom. As my critical consciousness is deepened, I find I am in a better position to act in ways that can begin to address social inequities in the school where I work. However, it is not always easy to be a teacher who uses theory. It takes a lot of energy and hard work to be seeking out other ways of seeing and doing things in my classroom and to be constantly thinking against the 'truths' of primary teaching. Often, my engagement with theory leads me to further questions, puts me in stuck places; there are no quick fix answers with this approach. Yet it is through my application of theory to my work in the classroom that I have found ways of queering, or troubling, my own and my children's understandings of gender.

In her book, *Gender trouble: feminism and the subversion of identity* (1990) Judith Butler developed the idea of the heterosexual matrix to describe the ways in which heterosexuality is constructed and maintained as the norm. I realised that this matrix is being created and maintained each day in my classroom through interactions between myself, the teaching assistants and the children. Actions and events which seem insignificant become the sites where this happens, from where the children sit on the carpet, to who interrupts lessons to who plays kiss chase in the playground and how; from the coat colours worn by the children to the language I use to address them, to the presentation of homework. In these everyday, mundane moments of life in my classroom, the children and staff, including myself, are creating and policing what it means to be a boy or a girl.

Thinking back over my earlier endeavours to put gender and sexualities equalities on the agenda in the curriculum I delivered during my first year with *No Outsiders*, I question the extent to which the project-type approaches I at first adopted can ever succeed in troubling the everyday moments that create the matrix. For example, I taught a literacy unit on alternative fairy tales during which, among other interventions, I dressed up and performed in the role of a lesbian Cinderella character, seemingly troubling the children's assumptions about who it is possible to be in the classroom (see Chapter 7). Although it was undoubtedly exciting and engaging, the possibilities offered by such a teacher-led, planned initiative are limited. Here I describe my attempts to turn my attention to smaller interventions that might hold greater potential to question heterosexual norms in the classroom. My intention was to trouble the children's, and possibly my own, assumptions about gender binaries and open up discussion of the gender categories and inevitable hierarchies that were operating. What follows is my account of the instance, as written up on our project website, and the replies to it.

My initial website posting

We were doing addition and subtraction and I was getting my higher ability children to try to prove or disprove various statements (such as 'when you add 7 units to a number ending in 5 units, the answer always ends in 2 units'). I was preparing sheets with such statements for the lesson, and intended to draw people with speech bubbles with 'Fred thinks ... ' and then have the person saying the statement – just to make it a little more interesting for the kids. As I began to draw a boy with spiky hair I decided instead to make it a girl. I think the main difference between making the person male or female was the eyelashes (and the name).

When the children saw the sheet they remarked about the person I had drawn. One girl asked me, 'Did you draw that?' but after that they got on with the work without further comment, as far as I was aware. The following day we repeated the activity, this time with subtraction statements. This time I drew a person that looked, in conventional terms, unmistakably like a girl, but I called the person James. The children could not get their heads around it. One boy asked if he could cross the name out and change it to a girl's name. I asked why he wanted to do that. 'Because it's not a boy!' he replied. 'How do you know?' I asked. 'Because he is wearing a bow in his hair!' 'But can't boys wear bows in their hair?' I asked. The group of six children laughed and told me, no, boys can't wear bows in their hair, and I asked them, 'Why not?' The boy who had wanted to change the name told me, 'Boys wear bows around their necks, not on their heads.' I replied that I had never heard of anything like that and that I thought anyone could wear a bow wherever they liked! And I went off to attend to another group doing a different activity.

At the end of the lesson, I noticed that the girl who had asked me about yesterday's drawing had crossed out the name James on her sheet and written her own name (although the person I had drawn looked nothing like her). I didn't have a chance to speak more to the children about this ...

Elizabeth A's response

I think this is a really interesting example of queering the classroom through making a really simple move which leads to the creation of what Deb (Deborah Youdell – a member of the university team) would call an unintelligible body. And the fact that you expressed surprise to the children about that combination not being possible adds to its power as a queer act. It reminds me of something I was told once, about a pre-school worker: when he found the children dividing themselves into boys' tables and girls' tables, he went to them and asked, 'I'm a boy-girl: where do I sit?'

Here too, the simple act of disrupting recognised patterns required the children to think about how to take on this new impossible body. Unfortunately, I don't know how the children responded – but surely it must have made them think!

My response to Elizabeth A

But if the bodies are unintelligible, and thus perceived as impossible bodies – which I agree they were – how does it queer the classroom? Over time, perhaps, along with lots of other challenges to the kids' thinking and work on gender and sexuality? I guess it compelled them to justify what had been previously taken for granted – i.e. boys wear bows round their necks but not in their hair. And in doing that perhaps other possibilities were glimpsed as they were being dismissed …

Going beyond momentary troubling – thoughts on where to take queer practice from here

So, if the queering in these episodes has been momentary and the children have resisted, what next? How could this be followed up in a classroom? The demands of the numeracy lesson I was teaching meant that I could not take the time to unpack the children's responses with them. I could have questioned them further about why they thought only girls could wear bows in their hair, what they thought it would mean for a boy to wear a bow in

his hair and whether their thoughts about boys with bows in their hair were similar to their thoughts about girls with bows around their necks. I might have encouraged the children to engage further with the ideas by giving them materials to make bows themselves, which they could try on around their necks and in their hair. Perhaps the children could have tried to make other characters that troubled understandings of gender.

There are myriad ways in which this momentary act of queering could have been taken up and explored further. Some kind of follow-up would have given the children more space to think through their initial reactions to these impossible boy-girls on their numeracy worksheets. The challenge is finding the space to fit in such impromptu, non-curriculum driven learning into the already bursting school timetable. Non-recognisable within assessment for learning driven outcomes, these queer endeavours have to be pursued in moments when learning is not so formally scrutinised. For example, in PSHCE (personal, social, health and citizenship education) lessons, which are expected to be taught but not monitored or measured to the same extent as literacy, numeracy or science. Finding the time and space to engage in the thinking and action of queer pedagogies is not easy, yet it is through the take-up of such post-

structuralist theoretical tools that I am able to consider and question, and occasionally interrupt, the process of the construction of heterosexuality as the norm in my classroom.

Coming out at school
Andrew

I joined my current school in January 2001 to run the nurture group, which addresses the social and emotional needs of children in the school. I came out to the staff within my first week there and encountered no negative reactions from adults in the school. It was always assumed, however, that the children need not know about my sexual orientation. Is it relevant to my job? Not really, I thought. Every so often the children would ask, 'Are you married?' to which I would reply, 'I'm far too young to be married!' and that would be an end to it.

Over the years, my role and the role of the nurture group developed. I began to write emotional literacy plans and eventually a scheme of work which encouraged the children to be honest about their feelings (see Chapter 7 for examples). I began to feel I was acting dishonestly in these

lessons, because I was encouraging the children to talk and open up while I remained closed and secret.

I was also aware of some children for whom school was an utterly isolating experience. I wanted to be a good solid role model for any child who might need one. I first talked with my head teacher about coming out in 2004. He always said he would support the move, but many teachers at the time thought it a bad idea. People were afraid of bad reactions from some of the children and parents. For the next couple of years I had the odd moment where I thought, 'I'm going to come out!' but then didn't. One teacher always argued that I should; she would say, 'How are the attitudes of the children going to change unless they have a role model to challenge their thinking?' Twice she called me to her class during PSHE (personal, social and health education) lessons when the children were discussing sexuality and saying they didn't know any gay people. She would ask the children if they thought she might be gay. They would gasp and say, 'Of course not!' She'd respond with, 'How do you know?' and they'd ask, '*Are* you gay, Miss?' She'd say, 'I might be gay. The point is, it doesn't matter, does it?' She argued that the children needed to know a gay teacher to challenge the negative views they had about what a gay person was. I knew she was right, but it was all right for her – she was straight!

In 2006, my partner and I had a civil partnership and all the teaching staff and some lunchtime supervisors came to the evening reception. A teacher told me a parent had asked her, 'Is it true Mr X is getting married? What's his partner's name? I want to send him a card'. The teacher had panicked and replied, 'I'm not sure, I'll find out for you,' and run off.

> I never thought I'd be doing assemblies on my civil partnership. But I sort of made that pledge to some of the other same sex parents that I would talk about my civil partnership when it came round. When it did, I thought well either I just forget about it or do it. Everywhere I walk in school now a child wishes me well for my wedding!

That was the moment I knew I had to come out. Parents were going to find out, and I would rather be in control of the information than have rumours spreading. And I didn't want there to be the slightest suggestion that I was in any way ashamed, or that I was hiding my sexual orientation – even though I had been hiding it for the last five years. So I went round the whole staff and said, 'From now on if anyone asks, please say, 'Yes, he's getting married to his partner David'.' That afternoon, another teacher was asked, 'Is it true Mr X is getting married? What's her name?' and replied, 'It's not a woman. It's a man, he's called David'. The parent paused five seconds while the realisation sunk in and then said, 'Oh! Good on him!' and walked off.

That was a Friday afternoon, and I spent the weekend convinced that I was going to arrive on Monday to a gaggle of parents outside the school with placards. How ignorant and arrogant I was! I assumed a) that the parents would be talking about me all weekend, and b) that they would all be

> I talked to my head teacher again about coming out; I was terrified. I could talk with my head teacher about why I should come out for hours, but I still couldn't imagine actually doing it. (Andrew)

homophobic! I was the bigot! There was not a single reaction on the Monday. I stood on the playground welcoming children in and there was no change from the usual, 'Morning!' This gave me huge confidence in coming out to the children. I wanted to do it quickly; I was getting married in five days! But it still took me two more days to pluck up the courage.

I came out on Wednesday afternoon in a Year 5 pupils (age 9-10) circle time. I read a story called *Dougal's Deep Sea Diary* by Simon Bartram, which is about a man who goes to work every day and doesn't tell anyone that he goes deep sea diving at the weekend. I talked about how strange it was that all his friends at work thought they knew him, but actually they didn't know about the one thing that made him happy! 'Do you think he should tell them?' I asked. 'Would they change their minds about him if they knew? Do you think they would still like him?' Then we played a truth game where we all made three statements; two had to be lies and one had to be the truth. Everyone read out their statements and the class had to try and identify which of them were true. On my turn I said, 'I have four sisters, I was born in Australia, I'm getting married at the weekend'. A child immediately said, 'You're getting married!' to which I replied, 'Yes I am, to my partner, David. Your turn!', looking at the child next to me, who continued the game. There was a slight pause, and I heard a boy whisper, 'Is he gay?' and another answer, 'Yes. Shhhh,' and the game continued.

That was at 2:30 and by 3:15 the news was all around the school. Most of the teachers told me that children came up to them that afternoon and asked either, 'Is it true Mr X is getting married to a man?' or, 'Is it true Mr X is gay?' They all answered, 'Yes!' following it up with something like, 'It's great, isn't it! I love weddings'. The answers modelled to the kids what response was appropriate. No-one was embarrassed or uncomfortable. We modelled acceptance.

Since coming out, I feel transformed. I am fully confident in my role as a teacher who happens to be gay. I talk periodically to the children about where I went with my partner at the weekend, or where we are going on holiday. It's now two years since I came out. Last term a Year 5 (age 9-10) teacher told me a child in her class corrected her because she was talking

> The children in class are now aware of my partner, Martin, and know that I am married to a man and that I love him. We have since had discussions when the children want to talk about my 'husband'. I refer to Martin regularly, especially when recounting weekend/holiday activities.
> (Jon)

about growing up and being in a relationship and had only mentioned a heterosexual model. A child put his hand up and said, 'Miss, you can have boys falling in love with boys and girls falling in love with girls too'. We are reaching the stage in school now where being gay is understood and accepted.

Recently two of the parents at my school got married. The wedding was held at the church in the middle of the estate and the reception at the pub around the corner from the school. At school I was more out and proud than ever before, but here in the pub I felt like a fish out of water. Here I felt utterly vulnerable. There is a clear line drawn around my school. Inside it people generally don't make homophobic

> The project has also tapped into the latent anger I felt growing up gay and coming out in my late teens: the anger I felt then, and feel now, at the injustices we still have to fight against and the equality we still have to fight for. Perhaps when we as teachers can discuss LGBT issues in the same way as we discuss any other, perhaps when I can walk down the street holding my partner's hand or kiss him without looking around to assess the danger of doing so, then maybe my anger will begin to lessen.
> (John)

remarks, and when they do it is seen as unacceptable. In the pub, 25 metres away from that invisible line, the ethos is completely different.

I felt I had a huge neon sign over my head saying, 'I'M GAY!' Suddenly I regretted being so out at school. I think my school has become a bit of a bubble, a safe haven for me, which is an achievement in itself. Maybe it's time to work on the pub!

Coming out as trans in the primary classroom
Jay

This is an extract from a conversation between Jay, Elizabeth A and Renée. Jay had just been at a session with Year 6 pupils (age 10-11) where he talked about being a trans man, as part of the class's focus on identity. He had been working for a week in three of the project's schools: see Chapter 7 for Jay's planning and guidance notes.

I was really nervous on Sunday night, to the point where I had knots in my tummy. But as soon as I acknowledged that I didn't know how it was going to pan out, I allowed myself to relax. And I realised after the first session on the Monday that I needed to come out as trans, because it felt like there was something empty and something missing. Even though we'd had a lot of conversations about should I, shouldn't I, I thought, 'Well, you wouldn't stop a black person coming into the room and talking about their sense of identity and sense of self if you are doing a project on identity.'

Respond positively to children who wish to behave in ways typically associated with another gender. Allow children to decide how they express their gendered identities and support them in this. (Laura: Objectives from draft gender equality scheme action plan)

My gender identity was important, so I decided I was going to put it in the room the next day, and this is what I did. We were doing self-portraits and identifying the gender we were assigned at birth, and I said, 'Here is my self-portrait. I was assigned female at birth.' Long pause. And then, 'I like football and some masculine things and some girlish things as well.'

I was thinking that I will answer people's questions, and if they are personal we can have a conversation about whether that's something I'm not going to answer, or whether actually it would be useful. It's a bit like people wanting a piece of you, you know. But just because you want to know me, do I want to give myself? I want to educate you and I want the world to be a better place, but does that mean I have to tell you all of my own stuff? My God, is that what it takes?

I talk to the kids about how you can be boyish and a girl and you can be girlish and a boy, but it's a bit hard to be a girlish boy because that makes things difficult. My bottom line is that boys are oppressed to

Jay demonstrates a pupil's
self-portrait

> I've never done anything like this before. I don't think anyone else in the UK has. It's good to say okay, what's the actual picture here, I feel a bit funny so let's work out why. And it's like actually you are doing something very challenging and I feel like a pioneer, I really do, I am not being dramatic but that's how it feels. (Jay)

the point where they can't move, they can express hardly anything about their gender identity. For girls, there is a lot more room for expression and diversity, but for boys, the aggression of gender identity comes out more, so boys are aggressively boyish: everything is a lot more heightened.

At the moment, I don't think school is a gender variant safe space. We are living in a culture and time where it's very difficult to not be specifically boyish. If you are a girl and you are not very girlish that's also quite difficult, but it's far more of a problem to be a sissy, a wuss. It's embodied, it's not

> I told the class that 'sissy' was used to describe me in a very negative way when I was at school because I didn't like doing the things that boys are 'supposed' to like doing: I played with the girls, I enjoyed so-called girls' games and activities such as skipping and sewing. (John)

conscious: it's repeated, deeply, culturally. It's been quite a sad week in those terms, coming to this realisation and thinking no wonder the trans women I see and the young people I come across have such a complex relationship to their own sense of self. It's quite depressing; their education has not been healthy and safe. It's really emotional to just accept that. So we need some really good work to open that up.

And I introduce the term gender neutral: you can like gender neutral things and you can also look or be gender neutral. I introduce a couple of people whose gender you can't really tell, and ask, 'Is it OK not to know what gender they are?' 'Yeah, it's OK.' And if, for example, a girl wants to show everyone her self-portrait, and she was assigned female at birth and everything on the page is hyper girly, that's fine as well. I wouldn't want to deter her from being girly or girlish.

What we understand trans to be is limited by its representation in the media, which is obsessed with surgery, but I see my job as saying that trans is a spectrum, it's about lots of things. Why should it be such a big deal to ask people to tell us what pronoun they prefer and what their chosen name should be? There is this idea that they would change it every day! But if all my life I've been 'she', for want of a better expression, and I say, 'Actually I'm Jay now and I prefer to use the 'he' pronoun,' if

> It's about our identity, it's not about getting rid of any of that. It's about opening it up and saying you can have more if you want, and you can contradict yourself if you want and you can change your mind in ten years time if you want to do something different. (Jay)

people refuse to do that or they are not really trying, there's a tension there, and at some point I'm going to say, 'Can you get my pronoun right, please?' I'm going to make that demand. But for the time being, if I know you are trying and you are giving it your best, why should I have anger towards you? It's about human interaction.

Talking about trans: learning from children's responses
Jo, Katie and Karen

Jo is the head of a school where several teachers were closely involved in the project. She asked these teachers to coordinate the input from visiting project facilitators. But there was one condition: when Jay came in to work with Katie's class, she didn't want him to come out as a trans man ... They talked about this to Elizabeth A and Renée later that week.

Jo: I didn't want Jay to be open about being transgender; I felt that at this stage in the school's involvement in the project it would be too big an issue to address. I just wanted him to come in and talk about gender. So we made that agreement, and Jay was comfortable with that, as far as I was aware. But in Jay's discussion with Year 6 (age 10-11) somebody asked a question about 'transvestites', so Jay discussed cross dressing and transsexuals and apparently, there was just a look between Katie and Jay, and Katie's look back said, 'OK, I am really nervous, I haven't got a clue what Jo is going to say to this, but go for it.' And he did.

Katie: Jay stood there and read out from his self-portrait, 'When I was born I was assigned female at birth.' And it just went deadly silent; I've never heard them that quiet. And I was just thinking, 'Oh my God, what is going to happen next?' And then he read out something else and it was almost like they were like, 'Oh, right.' And as soon as he'd said that, I was thinking, 'Oh, no, no, no, I am so in trouble.' But then when I listened to the discussion they had with

him, I've never felt so proud to be a teacher in my life.

The children were just amazing. They were asking him things like, 'So do you feel happier now you are a boy?' And then they asked him things like, 'So if you were a girl how come you've got a beard?' And Jay said, 'I inject myself with testosterone.' And they were like, 'Oh, you have to inject yourself.' But they weren't bothered, you know, it was the idea that he had to inject himself that got the first negative reaction.

Jo: That was just before lunchtime. Katie came to see me and said, 'I don't want you to panic but ... ' And I thought, 'Oh, my God, no ...' But Katie said, 'Before you start, it was right. I felt completely comfortable about it. I was nervous about it, my heart was in my mouth ... ' And she was glowing, her eyes were sparkling, and she said, 'If you get any parents coming in, if anything comes back to you about this in the school, I will stand by your side and tell them that it was absolutely the right thing, it was perfect timing and the children's response was stunning.'

> One boy decided to dress up as a girl on Comic Relief day: the theme of the day was Dare to be Different. He changed his name to Nicola and wore a dress and hair clips all day. No one said anything negative. I made sure that he won the prize for best-dressed boy of the day when all the children paraded in assembly.
> (John)

And then I thought, 'Do you know what, it would have been a bloody shame if he'd been in school and he hadn't talked about himself.' So after lunch, I decided to go into the class and ask the children about the session. And I was just blown away by what they said. It ranged from, 'What's the big issue?' to one girl saying, 'How brave was he to stand up in front of us and say that!' And I said, 'Why was he brave?' And she said, 'Well, you know, it took a lot of courage to say that to us when he didn't know how we'd respond.'

Karen: I'm a parent here as well as a teacher: my daughter's in the Year 6 class that Jay worked with. That day, she came to see me in school and said, 'Do you know Jay?' and I said, 'Yes,' and she said, 'Well, that dude is a girl.' And I said, 'Well, no, he's not, he's a man.' And she said, 'No, he's a

Pupils working with Jay on their multi-media self-portraits

girl.' And I said, 'No, he's not. Why do you keep saying he's a girl?' And she said, 'I've been speaking to him. He said, "I was born a woman." He didn't make it very clear whether he'd had the op or not but he injects himself with testosterone and so now he lives as a man.' So I said, 'He lives as a man, so he's a man.' And she said, 'Yeah.' So I asked, 'Is he a man?' and she said, 'Yeah,' and then toddled off. I think she just came to see what my reaction would be, and also to check what her own thinking was, to sound out what was what. That was a few days ago. I asked her last night what her favourite thing had been this week. She's quite arty, so I expected it to be an art thing, but she said, 'When Jay came in.'

Jo: I've had two lots of feedback from parents. One is from one of my support staff whose daughter is in Year 6. The daughter went home and told her mum and dad all about Jay. She said, 'OK, mum, when he was born he was assigned female, but he didn't feel comfortable in himself about living his life as a female. And now he's had an operation and he's living life as a man and he's got a partner ... ' And her mum said she was horrified at first, but when she got to the end of listening, she just thought, 'She is so comfortable with what she is saying and she is so articulate and so knowledgeable. How do you argue with that?'

And another parent who is a governor and has a daughter in Year 6 told me her daughter had gone home and done exactly the same. And she's a child who's got learning difficulties, she's a very introverted girl who doesn't actually say a lot, she'd gone home and said virtually the same to her mum. And she'd said, 'Do you know what? That's going to stay with me for the rest of my life.'

But the language that came out of it! I was having lunch in the dining hall with Year 5 (age 9-10) and I said to some of the girls, 'So how did your session go?' And it was absolutely fascinating. One girl said to me, 'Are you gender specific, Mrs X?' And I said, 'Actually, do you know what? I am very girly but I love Formula One racing, so what does that make me?' And another girl said that she was gender neutral. I just look at children in a completely different way now, because of the impact it's had on how they are talking.

And I just think how fortunate our children are that they have had this opportunity. This is about developing their well-being and their personal development, this is bog-standard stuff. It really is. It doesn't feel whacky and way out now. It really doesn't. It doesn't feel like that for any of us now.

Shifts in staff attitudes
Andi

Andi's school was planning its upcoming inclusion week in February 2008. Initially the school intended to approach inclusion/equality/diversity by each class exploring a different country, under the title 'It's a wonderful world.' This would have made it difficult to explore sexualities as part of inclusion. The following is from a series of emails from Andi to Elizabeth A.

5 December

Had a meeting with the staff ... We talked about the wonderful world theme for our inclusion week, and I expressed my concerns about the international focus emphasising an 'us and them' mentality about diversity and difference. For this I got bombarded with, 'But they are different, that's what diversity is.' I give up. I said there was the Harvey Milk book that would be good for upper Key Stage 2, and so on, to which the responses were along the lines of, 'Well I'm not sure ... I would have to be confident delivering it.'

6 December

Hi, further developments! After a semi-heated discussion yesterday I returned to school to find the head saying that she had rethought the whole idea and that it won't be 'A wonderful world' after all, but instead, 'It's good to be different,' which will allow access to all inequalities. I was pleased in a way that she considered how I had felt about it all, and that I'd said what I had. So I think we will go with the country theme in the mornings of that week and discussion on religion, gender, race etc. in the afternoons. One really good thing is that everyone has taken a project book to look at to see how they can fit it in with that week: the books are out of the box and spread on our large staffroom table so you can't help but notice them. Still a bit safe as the ones chosen have a general equalities theme rather than focusing specifically on sexualities, but things are afoot to change.

9 January, after the Christmas break

This is unbelievably FANTASTIC! There is so much happening that I just don't know where to start! The staff are totally buzzing with ideas about what to do. There's one member of staff who wouldn't even read the books properly before. She is now using *Daddy's Roommate*, because she thinks it's best to go in full on! As well as using *While You Were Sleeping* (about which she said, 'I'm not sure I can read it without crying'), she is basing her entire planning on weddings, using the civil partnerships pictures in *We Do*. She's going to scan a few and blow them up on the interactive whiteboard, and discuss them,

'It's good to be different...'

and then show other weddings around the world! W – O- W! This is with Year 5 (age 9-10).

I think everyone went home yesterday with at least three books to use or get ideas from. Two staff asked for some advice … it's just so unbelievable … One colleague even said, 'I wish we were doing the whole *No Outsiders* thing now instead of having an international focus'! I mean, what can I say! AND the project books are going to be totally embedded not only into our new creative curriculum but also into our literature spine of particular books for this year's Year of Reading… The SAME BOOKS that you were asked to remove from the school not three months ago! I feel so, so invigorated by this new change of perception by the staff, and I do mean that sincerely, that everyone is being really interested and almost driven!

Meeting challenges; maintaining professionalism
John

> I think equality of any sort is the most important area I need to teach. Oh, and yeah, I'm scared – it's what makes me realise it's worth doing. Without fear I wouldn't find a solution to stop me, or others, being so scared, ever again! (Andi)

When our school governors were introduced to the project – which would eventually include the *Tango* opera – and our forthcoming training with Mark, one of the parent governors, who's known for her tendency to misinterpret information, told parents in the playground that I was going to be 'teaching gay sex in Year 1.' This governor has since avoided meetings where anything 'contentious' or 'controversial' was to be raised and has now, in fact, left the school. She was also on the parent council, where she told a member who is also a teaching assistant at the school that she felt she couldn't express her opinion for fear of being labelled homophobic.

After this incident, a small group of Year 1 parents who gather at the school gates asked our Office Administrator if she 'was married to a man or a woman' and asked our Year 1 teaching assistant whether she was a lesbian. The TA was upset and complained to the head, and the parents were required to apologise to the TA in the head's presence.

> I read five of these books. They were nothing like I imagined they'd be. I would have no problem with my children reading these books, even though I was quite concerned at first. My daughter has read them all and really enjoyed the stories. My other daughter has read two and enjoyed those. (Andi's colleague)

The training day took place as planned, however, and a good time was had by all! It felt really good to be dealing with this subject out in the open and with all teaching staff. A member of staff who, we felt, had been a little resistant to the issues dealt with during the day said afterwards that it had been the most useful training she'd had since being at the school and that she'd thoroughly enjoyed the day.

Talking across cultures
Zoë, Nikki and colleagues

In February 2008, some of the parents at two of the project schools near each other in the city objected strongly to aspects of the project's work. Rumours and misunderstandings quickly spread about what the schools were doing. We held several meetings with parents both before the project work started and after parents had voiced their concerns, so we could discuss and clarify any misconceptions on both sides. The piece below is divided into two sections: an extract from an article written by Renée and Elizabeth A for the local LGB Forum journal in response to the situation, followed by extracts from a conversation between four members of the project team immediately after a meeting attended by over 70 parents.

Extract from local LGB Forum article by Renée and Elizabeth A

Recent events in two project primary schools have sent a wave of concern across the LGBT community, both locally and nationally, about the status of LGBT equality work in education, and LGBT equality more broadly. Anxiety and anger expressed by certain parents about the schools' use of children's books featuring LGBT characters and lesbian and gay headed families caused protests at the schools. At the Council's behest, the books were withdrawn from the two schools to allow for a cooling-off period while consultations took place. Consultations with the schools, the Council and local community groups about how to proceed are still going on. Feelings on all sides continue to run high and we have not yet reached a resolution. What has caused such a stir is that the protests came from a group of Muslim parents, led by Muslim community leaders.

But this controversy is not about Islam. As members of the LGBT community know, opposition can come from any quarter, and there are LGBT people and heterosexual supporters of LGBT people who are of all faiths and none, just as there are opponents to LGBT equality of all faiths and none. Wherever we have met opposition, whether from individuals or, as here, from a particular group, the objections have been largely based on misunderstandings of two kinds: the first is about the legal and moral right of LGBT people to live and grow up experiencing affirmation and respect. The second is about the way in which work which addresses equality, whether on the basis of race, disability, sexual orientation or anything else, must always be proactive and positive, and not simply wait to respond to prejudice. Any work which breaks new ground is sometimes met with misunderstanding and even hostility, but dealing with these reactions *is* the work of the project. What we are aiming to do is to make a real difference to the inclusion of LGBT equality in the broad spectrum of equality work within schools.

Discussion between Zoë, Nikki (both based in one of the protesting schools), David (the project's regional research assistant for the area) and Elizabeth A immediately after a meeting attended by over 70 parents:

At the meeting, strong views were expressed for and against the project's work. Interpreters translated for those for whom English was not a first language.

Elizabeth: So how do you think the meeting went this morning?

Zoë: I think it was what I was expecting. I thought it was really good that the parents had an opportunity to hear our point of view, and they listened. But I feel that there is a massive, massive closing of ears by some parents and that whatever we say they just don't want this to happen. There is definite homophobia there. You can say it's for religious beliefs but to me, it's homophobia. They don't like it and I find that really disappointing.

David: But it's now, it's there, it's out in the open and even in that discomfort you can say actually we know what we are dealing with now.

Zoë: But it's not OK. It makes me feel sick. I feel like I've just been to a BNP meeting or something. I just won't have people assert their right and power over another group, it makes me feel horrible. It's just horrible. And it's worrying in terms of our future

relationship with the parents, which doesn't mean that I wish we weren't doing it at all or weren't having those conversations, but I guess that I've seen a side of some parents that I really wish I hadn't seen. And I don't want to know about how they feel about gay people really because it's actually really unpleasant.

Elizabeth: It's so useful for me to hear that. As somebody who is in a lesbian relationship I kind of think well, of course I've got to accept that some people hate me. Some of these people are going to hate me, or they would if they knew. And just to hear somebody with a completely objective view saying, 'That makes me really feel sick' makes me feel really touched. But it's also really important. Because there is a tendency I think, if you are gay or lesbian, to think well, we've got to accept a certain amount of homophobia as a cultural and natural necessity of life. And you are saying no, we haven't.

> I draw parallels with race equality work, saying that when we tackle racism we are both reactive and proactive. We react and deal with incidents as they arise, but we would never have made much progress for black and minority ethnic communities without all the crucial proactive work. (Sue K)

Zoë: No, we haven't. You know, it's just about equality, isn't it. And it used to be that people thought the same thing about racism. When people first came over here from the Caribbean, they kind of accepted that there were some places that wouldn't accept black tenants, that they would be called names, and so on.

Elizabeth: When I was talking to one of the mothers after the meeting, in the middle of all her complaints about the children being too young, they couldn't understand and so on, she slipped in, 'One of my friends is a lesbian.' So I said, 'Well, what does she think about the project?' and she looked quite taken aback and said, 'I haven't asked her.' And I said, 'Well, go and ask her and see what she thinks.' So she is saying, 'I am a Muslim, and speaking as a Muslim I think this is inappropriate,' but at the same time, she's saying, 'One of my friends is a lesbian'! But I think that kind of alliance is very useful.

Nikki: The whole argument of them saying the children were too young was because they immediately think about sexual activity. But it's not about that at all [see Chapter 7 for our teaching plans]. I think it was a very well managed meeting on the whole, but I just think there's still a lot of confusion, a lot of fear. You know, we never expected to change their views. It was just something to make them think about their own beliefs and it's planted the seed.

> One boy sent me a card when he left school saying, 'Thank you for helping me see things in a different way'. I have blu-tacked that card to the wall in my office and look at it when I'm feeling down about the prejudices that I occasionally encounter. (John)

Elizabeth: I did feel that there was a range of different groups represented there. And looking across and seeing the expressions on people's faces, it certainly was very far from being all negative. And within the Muslim group of parents there were quite a lot of agreeing nods when points were being made by the project team.

Zoë: And also really good listening from a group of mums who come along to everything and they are really supportive parents, and I think there is a lot of trust there. And although they are probably not going to come out openly in support – that's a step too far – I feel that they trust us as educators to do the right thing with their children to an extent.

NIKKI: It's like if we had a core group of parents who were all members of the BNP, you know, saying that they didn't want their children celebrating Eid or being part of an assembly that is discussing religion.

ZOË: That's exactly the same. And that's why I had this distaste coming away from it because I really don't want to hear homophobic points of view. Because it's just really unpleasant, you know, from people that I say good morning to and hug quite often. Do you know what I mean? It's just horrible.

The situation in these schools remained tense throughout the project, but although solutions have not yet been found, many moves have been made to strengthen communications across cultural boundaries (the schools already had a good relationship with their local community) and to enable voices to be heard -from both the local Muslim community and the local LGB community – to ensure that people felt they were represented. New moves have since been made within the Local Authority to introduce LGBT equality teaching across the city's schools, and this has made the project schools feel less isolated.

Meeting challenges from the Christian Right
Kate

The following is taken from Kate's journal and emails to project team members, over a period of 5 months.

The governors' meeting went on until 9.30pm this week (it was meant to end at 8.30) because one governor was voicing objections to *No Outsiders* – and *all* the other governors spoke up for it, including two other evangelical Christian governors who believe homosexuality is wrong, but see the issue as being about an inclusive school and respecting difference. The governor who first objected would not be moved, though, so the head teacher immediately went into action, sending a letter to all parents about the project and inviting them to discuss any concerns at a series of meetings. The meetings were set in morning, afternoon and evening sessions so that all the parents could attend ...

* * *

We've now started an equalities group, whose members include the governor who had objected to the project and another parent who shares her views equally strongly. The core group planning the equalities meetings has agreed to principles for the meetings (see Chapter 6). They are that discussion or dissent should not be stifled, but that one or two individuals should not be allowed to prevent practical action of any kind. The tactics are to have a strong chairperson, to begin the meeting by agreeing on aims and objectives, if necessary passing them by majority vote, and then moving on to the practical things we can do. General discussion will be left to the last item on the agenda.

Perhaps we can find a way forward to work together, but it will need the two opponents of same sex relationships to realise that what we are trying to do is to be inclusive and supportive of all minority groups, not to promote homosexuality over all other lifestyles. This will require the rest of us to back down from seeing them as the enemy. It's so frustrating to have lots of people full of energy and enthusiasm blocked by two people who are there because they don't want same sex couples to be treated in the same way as others. They insist, of course, that they have nothing against homosexuals, but that they just don't want their children to hear any mention of them at their age. Substitute black. 'I have nothing against black people, it's just that I think children need to be older before they hear about them, and want the right to withdraw my child from any lesson where they might be mentioned.' Reasonable?

* * *

Another equalities and diversity meeting – another opportunity for the oppositional governor to inform us that we are 'promoting' homosexuality, that homosexuality is condemned by the Bible, and that children should not hear of such dreadful things as same sex partners. I now feel I am not being fair to the good people who have volunteered their time and effort to work for the school and the good of all the children who attend it. At each meeting they are having to listen to statements that they, or their friends, are not fit people to be even mentioned to children. Little wonder that several have said they are not sure they can continue to come, as it is too upsetting. Is it fair even to ask them? What a shocking waste of time and energy these fixed opinions are causing ...

* * *

Mark came to do some training on Wednesday, leading to interesting discussions with the dinner supervisors, interesting discussion with Year 6 (age 10-11) – and then came the equalities

meeting, which Mark also attended. A good turnout, with several people taking time off work to attend. It didn't take long for the governor to again declare her views and protest about the books being harmful because they present same sex couples; that this was confusing for children; that they are far too young etc. Then she brought the Bible out to back her – 'An abomination'? I think even Mark was a little taken aback ...

The head was at the meeting and next day she and the chair of governors asked the governor to see them, and told her that she could not be part of an equalities group when she did not believe in the equality of one of the groups which is specifically identified in the group's aims. The governor constantly cited the Bible to justify her position. The chair of governors at one point challenged her by saying the Bible also advocated stoning – presumably she didn't agree with that? To which she gave the classic reply: 'That was then, this is now ...'

* * *

Well, here's a surprise. The governor has decided to take her children to another school! This after she had another lengthy meeting with the head, this time accompanied by her husband. She was still wanting her child withdrawn from any situation where there might be mention of a same sex relationship – even if it was

I disliked the way religious views were reported [in the press] as being monolithically against teaching and learning tolerance. I am a straight, church-going father of three. I want my children to know that being cared for and loved is the birthright of all children, and that caring families and networks come in all shapes and forms. ('A straight, church-going father of three' in Edinburgh)

I believe that Jesus came to earth to die for us, for our sins, and the reason why He did that was because He loved people so much. And if He could do that, I don't see why people like us should go out just pointing fingers to say 'Ooh, you're not right'. (Teacher, North East)

between a couple of penguins – because it's her right to withdraw her child from sex education. The head wouldn't budge, would not agree that this was sex education, and said that she regularly mentioned families in assemblies, and would include same sex parents ... It's a shame to lose her two children, with another about to join next year – great kids, who have made good progress. It's also a shame to lose a parent who was involved in lots of groups – however, generally there's great relief (and some surprise) that the hours of pointless argument are over.

Points to remember when responding to challenges
Mark

■ If your LGBT equalities work is challenged, a useful technique is simply to question each assertion. WHY is *King and King* not age appropriate? (e.g. see Kate's and Leanne's uses of King and King in Chapter 3.) **How** is talking about gay people promoting homosexuality? (eg see 'Promoting equality – or gay sex?' in Chapter 1 and the numerous examples in Chapters 2-5.) **Why** is a comparison with, for example, refusing to talk about Islam in the context of promoting religious and cultural equality 'not the point'? (eg see Zoë and Nikki's discussion in Chapter 5.) **Who** are these young people who are being 'damaged' by the 'promotion' of homosexuality and/or gender variance? (eg see Jo, Katie and Karen's account in Chapter 5.)

This approach is effective because, firstly, it may cause those in opposition to reflect on their views; secondly, it may stop them making such unfounded and offensive comments in future and therefore save everyone a lot of upset, and thirdly, it will empower others to feel that they themselves are not being discriminatory in rejecting demands for teaching on LGBT equalities to be withdrawn or challenging objectors if their language or behaviour is inappropriate.

■ Point out to objectors that there will be children with LGBT parents or family members at your school – and that some of the children will themselves grow up to be LGBT. These children need to see positive representations of their lives just as much as everyone

> A parent governor who has objected to our work said to me recently that she 'doesn't have a problem with me'. I'm proud (and a little surprised) that I managed to maintain my professionalism by not retorting with something equally patronising or derogatory about her! (John)

else does. In the circumstances, not talking about LGB identities and relationships and varied gender expression would clearly be discriminatory.

■ A few other things which may help to convince doubters (or preserve your sanity!):

☐ Schools have a statutory duty to prevent all forms of bullying. You cannot prevent homophobic bullying without talking positively about LGBT identities and relationships – and the impact that discrimination has on LGBT people.

☐ Although most parents and carers now accept that schools will challenge racist attitudes robustly and consistently, some feel that attempts to promote LGBT equalities and challenge homophobia and transphobia in schools undermine their own values. However, schools cannot arrange themselves to suit particular individuals' or groups' value systems. Parents and carers have the right to promote whatever values they consider appropriate at home – but they cannot expect schools to uphold these values at the expense of others. Schools serve the whole community and as such need to be inclusive of all its members.

☐ A common objection to work on LGBT equalities is that it in some way 'promotes' homosexuality. Rather than getting drawn into discussion about whether it does or not, point out that heterosexuality is being promoted wherever we turn. Every story which features a child with a mum and dad (or in which a prince marries a princess) promotes heterosexuality. Including a few children with two mums or princes who fall for other princes is simply a small way of trying to redress the balance.

See also Mark's advice in Chapter 6 on developing aims for equalities work.

Supporting teachers

Annie

The following is a selection of excerpts from the borough-wide resource Annie developed as part of her involvement in No Outsiders. *Further extracts from the resource appear in Chapter 7.*

How to challenge homophobia

To challenge homophobia effectively, we need:

■ Continued professional development for *all* staff. This is vital – all those who work in schools need both knowledge and skills so they can effectively confront homophobia. Schools need to have the understanding and confidence to challenge the derisive use of language about sexual orientation and gender as rigorously as they would challenge the use of pejorative language around ethnicity or race. Don't assume that only LGBT staff are well placed to address such issues. It is they who often find this most difficult.

■ Peer support programmes. These can be highly effective. The opinions of older students frequently carry real weight with younger pupils. Peers can also support students whose choices may not conform to traditional gender stereotypes.

■ Recording incidents. One of the most useful activities a school can do is to audit their position by involving all members of the school community in recording homophobic incidents – anonymously if necessary. Such incidents should be given the same status, and dealt with and monitored in the same way as sexist or racist incidents.

■ Promotion of emotional health and well-being.

■ Using a whole school approach – see the School Self-Review below.

A note on language

Children often use the word 'gay' just to be negative. Though used derisively, it is seldom seen as homophobic because it is generally not directed at a person perceived to be homosexual. Pupils assume that teachers don't regard using the word as unacceptable because they don't challenge it. This is a particular problem in primary schools. Many children repeat language they pick up at home or from the television without really understanding what it means. All staff must think about the language they use, challenge what others say, if necessary and support pupils in reflecting on how stereotypes are built and sustained and how prejudice is manifest.

Such work should take place throughout the school whenever situations arise and not just in circle time or PSHE lessons. Stories are an excellent starting point for discussion in primary schools, which are seen as relatively safe settings compared to secondary schools. And if children are not encouraged to challenge their own prejudice and that of others at primary level, it is unlikely that this will happen later.

School Self-Review

Homophobia is best tackled by a whole school approach. You have to start from where your school is now. The National Healthy Schools Standard has identified ten areas in which action should be taken and which together will create a supportive ethos and shared ownership:

- Leadership, management and managing change

- Policy development

- Curriculum planning and resources

- Teaching and learning

- School culture and environment

- Giving pupils a voice

- Provision of effective support services

- Staff professional development, health and welfare

- Partnerships

- Assessing, recording and celebrating achievement

The NHSS self-review checklist will allow a school to audit its current position in relation to challenging homophobia. It can be found at www.wiredforhealth.gov.uk/word/checklist_04.doc

The following pre-training knowledge and skills questionnaire can be used for individual reflection, followed by group discussion.

Pre-training knowledge and skills questionnaire for primary school teachers

1) Have you received any equalities training before?

2) On a scale of 1 – 10, how would you score your knowledge on issues relating to lesbian, gay, bisexual and transgender (LGBT) people? (1=low, 10=high)

3) Do you believe it is important to specifically identify homophobic bullying in school bullying policies?

4) Are you aware of your school's policy on bullying? If so, how does homophobic bullying fit in?

5) Does your school have an equal opportunities policy for pupils? If so, does it incorporate LGBT issues?

6) Does your school have an equal opportunities policy for staff? If so, does it incorporate LGBT issues?

7) Are you aware of any incidents of homophobic bullying/homophobia that are occurring or have occurred in your school?

8) Do you monitor and record incidents of homophobic bullying and homophobia in your school?

9) What is your understanding of homophobia?

10) What is your understanding of heterosexism?

11) Are you aware of any UK legislation regarding homophobic behaviour?

12) What do you consider to be homophobic language?

13) Would you feel comfortable challenging the use of homophobic language or behaviour by a pupil or pupils in school?

14) Would you feel comfortable challenging the use of homophobic language or behaviour in school by a colleague?

15) Do any of your pupils use the word 'gay' to describe something or someone in a derogatory way?

16) What do you think the obstacles are to tackling issues around LGBT issues and homophobia in primary schools?

17) Do you believe that the pupils in your school have an understanding of LGBT issues?

18) Do you feel that primary schools are an appropriate setting for addressing issues affecting LGBT young people?

19) If yes, where in the curriculum do you think it is appropriate to discuss these issues?

20) Do you use any resources in the classroom that include or mention LGBT people?

   a) If so, please list them.

   b) If not, would you like information on the resources that are available?

21) Do you feel comfortable discussing issues around sexuality in school? If not, why is this?

22) What are you hoping to get personally out of the training?

> In ten years time when everybody is doing it then I am going to be really proud of myself to think I was one of the first people to be doing it. Because at the end of the day somebody has always got to go first and I am quite willing to put myself forward. (Leanne)

Legislation and rationale for governors
Katherine

Katherine presented the points below at a governors' meeting where the No Outsiders *project was being introduced. For information about legislation and government guidance, see Chapter 1.*

> Years ago one of the governors ran out of a governors' meeting crying because they were talking about boys being able to do domestic science and cookery and girls being able to do woodwork. Yesterday, she said how things have changed. (Jo)

Why we need to address homophobic bullying in primary school: A government perspective

Bullying: don't suffer in silence (DfES, 2002).

Homophobic bullying should be addressed in schools by

- including it in the school's anti-bullying policy – so pupils know discrimination is wrong and that the school will act

- covering it in professional development days on bullying in general

- guaranteeing confidentiality and appropriate advice to LGB pupils

Sex and relationships education guidance (DfEE, 2000)

- It is up to schools to make sure that the needs of all pupils are met in their programmes. Young people, whatever their developing sexuality, need to feel that sex and relationships education is relevant to them and sensitive to their needs

- The Secretary of State for Education and Employment is clear that teachers should be able to deal honestly and sensitively with sexual orientation, answer appropriate questions and offer support

- Schools need to be able to deal with homophobic bullying

- The government recognises that there are strong and mutually supportive relationships outside marriage

- Sex and relationships education policies should be inclusive of all pupils

- Having a sex and relationships education policy in line with this guidance will be a key part of meeting the criteria for sex and relationships education outlined in the National Healthy School Standard.

Every Child Matters – outcomes and aims:

■ Being physically and mentally healthy

– being sexually healthy

■ Staying safe, and being protected from harm and neglect

– safe from bullying and discrimination

■ Enjoying and achieving

– attending and enjoying school

■ Making a positive contribution by being positively involved in community and society

– developing positive relationships and choosing not to bully or discriminate

■ Achieving economic well-being

– engaging in further education, employment or training on leaving school

– achieving readiness for employment

Ofsted Self Evaluation Forms:

■ What is the overall effectiveness and efficiency of leadership and management?

■ How well is equality of opportunity promoted and discrimination tackled so that all learners achieve their potential?

■ To what extent do learners feel safe and adopt safe practices?

■ Do learners feel safe from bullying and racist incidents?

Why it's beneficial to be involved in this work:

■ In today's society everyone needs to have a basic understanding of differences in relationships and families in order to challenge prejudice. When we are better informed about difference, we can celebrate rather than belittle it.

■ By using materials that present positive images regarding race, gender, disability and sexual orientation, we help to ensure that the curriculum is made relevant for all.

I asked my children if they could imagine why teachers might be a bit reluctant to talk to young children about different types of family, for example, those with two mums or two dads. I said, 'I think some people believe that we should only teach children about the kind of family they think of as 'normal', that is one that has a mum and a dad'. My youngest daughter replied: 'But that would be really bad because if your family wasn't like that then you would think you didn't have a family. That would be horrible and make you feel really sad'. I hadn't made that leap from having your family identity ignored to having it totally negated. So, yet again, I learned something from my daughter, then 9 years old. (Teresa, a local authority advisor, after attending a project training day)

Do a parent meeting, Rachael!
Rachael

The Fear!

I had a meeting with the head teacher to discuss what our school was going to do in relation to the project. We reviewed the sex and relationships education policy, which the deputy had recently rewritten to include mention of the project, in reference to teaching about different sorts of relationships and family structures. It gave some ideas about what would be included in the teaching.

It was decided to hold a parent meeting for us to introduce the new policy. This was fine and I agreed it would be a good idea. Imagine my horror when my head said she felt I should say something. I am not a natural public speaker – I hate it and have avoided it my whole life. Saying a few words at a staff meeting fills me with fear, even in front of people I spend most of my time with! The idea that I was now going to address parents, Parent Teacher Association members and governors on a subject that could be sensitive was terrifying. I pulled myself together and thought, 'Well, it's just going to be a couple of minutes'. So I braced myself and started to feel fine about it.

Then I had another meeting with my headteacher. She asked me to prepare a Powerpoint presentation, and this set me panicking once more. It was changing gradually from what I thought was going to be a few words to a full-blown presentation and talk. On top of this, staff were asked to attend. I must remind you that it wasn't the subject that was frightening me – it was the audience.

I went home that night and began to prepare my presentation. I knew what I wanted to say and borrowed some of Mark's statistics. I convinced myself that I would get shouted down. My head teacher was brilliant and comforted me through my woes. She said she would stay with me during the whole thing – and that if I got stuck she would jump in!

I actually ended up feeling very disappointed, as not many parents turned up. Those who did were brilliant and were in full agreement with us educating children about LGBT issues. The only time the parents appeared shocked was when we gave them the statistic about the age at which children realised they were gay: 'youngest at 6, oldest at 13'. This statistic shocked me also – then I thought, how stupid – I had a boyfriend when I was 5!

Here is the Powerpoint presentation I prepared, with the support of Mark Jennett:

SEX AND RELATIONSHIPS EDUCATION (SRE) POLICY:

CARING FOR CHILDREN

- Within school we meet many standards to ensure the well-being of the children in our care.

- This includes all children, whatever their race, religion, abilities, whatever they think or say and whatever type of family they come from.

- We endeavour to protect them from any kind of harm, including bullying of any nature.

DfEE (Department for Education and Employment) 2000 GUIDANCE

- Our sex and relationships education policy is based on the DFEE document Sex and Relationships Education Guidance (2000).

- The guidance states that SRE is about 'understanding the importance of marriage for family life, stable and loving relationships, respect, love and care. It is also about the teaching of sex, sexuality and sexual health'.

NEW LEGISLATION

- To meet new guidelines from the government, schools must now be open to discuss same sex relationships with children when required.

- This does not mean promoting homosexuality. It means discussing it when needed at a level appropriate for the child.

GENERAL TEACHING COUNCIL FOR ENGLAND: CODE OF PROFESSIONAL VALUES AND PRACTICE

To ensure the positive development of individual pupils, teachers work within a framework of equal opportunities and other relevant legislation statutory guidance and school policies. Within this framework, teachers challenge stereotypes and oppose prejudice, to safeguard equality of opportunity, respecting individuals regardless of gender, marital status, religion, colour, race, nationality, class, sexual orientation, disability and age.

FAMILY DIVERSITY

- Children come from all sorts of families and we aim to make all of them comfortable to discuss their home life.

- This includes children who come from families where their parents are in same sex relationships.

- Within our PSHCME (personal, social, health, citizenship and moral education) lessons, children will be taught about various different family types. This may include families where there are two mums or two dads, in order to teach recognition and respect for others.

- Teaching at this school will always be relevant and appropriate to the age of the child.

CHALLENGING DISCRIMINATION

As part of our equality and inclusion policies, we are also dedicated to tackling any type of discrimination against others.

At our school this includes dealing with bullying of all types, including homophobic comments. It also includes challenging children when they use terms inappropriately.

BEATBULLYING STATISTICS

In a survey of primary and secondary school children conducted in 2006, over three quarters of the primary age children surveyed identified the use of the word gay as a way of attacking or making fun of someone.

NSPCC STATISTICS

- Calls about homophobic bullying accounted for 27% of the April 2006 calls to ChildLine relating to sexual orientation issues

- Boys account for 55% of the calls in this category, even though they represent only 25% of all calls to the helpline

- During April, 6% of calls relating to sexual orientation were from under 11s

FURTHER INFORMATION

- Further information is available in our SRE (Sex and Relationships Education) policy.

- You can read our policy in print or on the school website.

One parent said, 'We find the vocabulary quite inflammatory so could you do it without saying the word gay or homosexual?' And I said, 'Well, that would be like asking me to not mention the word black. It would be very tricky. I think I am beginning to understand what you are saying, those are very tricky words for you but actually we do need to use those words but we need to be sure that everybody understands what we mean.' (Head teacher, South West)

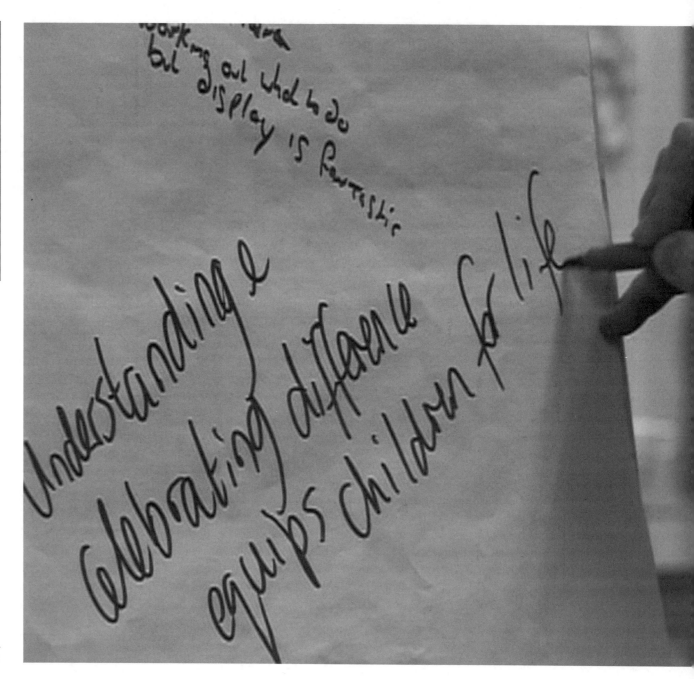

Responses to a family diversity exhibition

Preparing for family diversity fortnight
Nikki and Zoë

Zoë and Nikki organised a training day for staff and parents in preparation for a two-week focus on family diversity across the entire school. They prepared a Powerpoint presentation for the parents' meeting which portrayed images of a wide range of diverse family groups. The Powerpoint text is included below.

Outline of Families Fortnight Training Day

Message to staff:

During LGBT (Lesbian, Gay, Bisexual and Transgender) History Month (this February) we are planning to carry out a series of workshops with each class which aim to challenge gender stereotyping and introduce the concepts of different types of families and relationships, including same sex relationships.

All staff will attend a training session as follows. Staff will be divided between morning and afternoon sessions to ensure everyone can attend.

9.00 – 10.00

Meeting for parents to introduce plans for the work

10.45 -12.00

Training for Learning Support Assistants and teachers

Focus:

The impact of homophobia and gender stereotyping on children and young people

Legislation

Challenging homophobic language

Introducing the books that will be used in class

1.15 – 2.00

Training for School Meals Supervisory Assistants

2.00 – 3.15

Training for Learning Support Assistants and teachers

Focus of both sessions:

Challenging inappropriate/ homophobic language in the playground

> I think a lot of the No Outsiders work is about planting seeds for people that they might just come back to later on in their life and think, oh, that was portrayed in a positive kind of way, or I found out about it in school. (Miles)

Text of Powerpoint presentation for parents' meeting:

No Outsiders Fortnight – Family Diversity

What is a family? Can you draw it?

Family diversity

- Mixed race family
- Single parent family
- Step parents
- Blended family
- Foster family
- Adopted family
- Same sex parents

Children whose families are never talked about, who aren't represented in pictures can feel as though they don't exist or that they don't belong. We want to represent and include all types of families, people and relationships.

The law says that schools need to ensure that there is equality for all.

No Outsiders fortnight: 4 – 15 February

Each class will spend one morning or afternoon thinking about different kinds of families. The work is based on a collection of books. We will also have a visit from Dean Atta, a performance poet who will be working with Year 5 and 6 (ages 9-11).

What else would you like us to include about families?

Did you know that there are different people?

There are people who are gay

So don't take the mick, is that okay.

People who are lesbians have feelings too

But people still take the mick, men, women, maybe even you.

To be teased you must know what it feels like

So don't be rude to gays and lesbians, is that alright.

So don't be rude or racist to lesbians or gays

Just get along with each other and have a good play.

(Year 6 pupil's poem, written at home during Family Diversity Fortnight)

What do we do next? Training follow-up action plan
Sue K

Sue and her colleagues developed the following action plan after their training with Mark Jennett.

In too many schools homophobic attitudes among pupils often go unchallenged. The problem is compounded when derogatory terms about sexuality are used in every day language and their use passes unchallenged by staff. Where problems arise, staff have often had insufficient guidance on the interpretation of school values and what constitutes unacceptable language or values. (Ofsted Report on Sex and relationships Education, 2002)

■ Set out some procedures with set phrases and advice on challenging homophobic comments or language.

■ Develop an inclusive anti-bullying policy.

■ Audit our resources: what we have and how we use them at present.

■ Plan for purchase of inclusive resources including favourite *No Outsiders* books.

■ Review our curriculum. (This is part of our development plan).

■ Explore how we are working with families and community, and exactly what it is we are trying to work on with them.

■ Negotiate an agreement about how we present LGBT equalities work to children, families and colleagues.

■ Look at the DCSF *Safe to Learn* guidance on homophobic bullying (2007).

■ Review our planning proformas to include equalities links.

■ Develop a whole setting focus on challenging name-calling.

■ Set up a cross-setting working party to lead on this.

■ Review progress in 6 months.

Developing aims for LGBT equalities work
Mark

It is extremely helpful if work on LGBT equalities is clearly contextualised within the wider equalities agenda. It is vital that we are clear that we are talking about accepting difference, celebrating diversity, challenging prejudice, questioning stereotypes, treating everybody fairly and making everyone feel safe and included – as opposed to talking about sex or promoting homosexuality. Not only will it inform practice to ensure that talking about LGBT relationships becomes part of all the work a school does in personal, social, health and citizenship education (PSHE), social and emotional aspects of learning (SEAL), citizenship and elsewhere across the curriculum (see Chapters 2-5 and the planning in Chapter 7) but it will also help to make teachers feel safe and able to reassure and challenge any parents and carers who may have concerns about why the school is addressing these issues. (See also 'Promoting equality – or gay sex?' in Chapter 1).

Many schools involved in the *No Outsiders* project used it as an opportunity to review all their work on equalities to ensure that it was effective across the whole diversity spectrum – to make sure for example that they were challenging homophobia and sexism as effectively as they were addressing racism or discrimination directed at people with disabilities. Some key principles can be helpful:

- Develop a mission statement or statement of aims for your equalities work across the school, or for your equalities group if you are forming one. It should express what promoting equality and diversity means for you. This could usefully be based on existing school rules and policies that are familiar to everyone. Think about

  - how the school should feel safe and welcoming to everybody

  - how we all have the right to feel good about ourselves – and to see ourselves and our families represented across the school

  - how we should be kind to people who are different from ourselves

and not do things which might make them feel excluded

☐ how we are all unique and special and how this is something to be celebrated and enjoyed

■ Think about specific practical things you can do to achieve these aims. A couple of examples could be

☐ regularly reviewing all your policies (not just Equal Opportunities) to ensure that they are inclusive of – and help to promote equality for – all members of the community

☐ indentifying areas which are weaker than others – and deciding how to address them. For example, while staff may be confident about challenging racist remarks they may need additional support about how they can approach sexism. Similarly, the school may be delivering excellent work on ethnic diversity but neglecting to address sexual orientation – you may need to look at curriculum and resources to ensure that this is proactively included alongside other work on diversity

Pupils celebrate with a carnival at the end of a diversity focus week to complete a years's activities

We recognise that the children at our school live, and will live, in many different family situations and we aim to present different perspectives of family life through our curriculum. We will always challenge homophobic language. (Laura: extract from school equalities policy)

■ Include a clear definition of discrimination – both direct and indirect. Again, keep this simple. Direct discrimination might entail bullying people or leaving them out of something because of their difference; indirect discrimination could be failing to challenge or report such behaviour. Both should be identified as wrong. It can be helpful to produce a (non-exhaustive) list of the groups whose equality you wish to promote as part of your statement of aims, and include LGBT people or sexual orientation and gender expression in the list. This is important because it will make it clear why discrimination on these grounds has no place in your school. Broadly speaking, primary legislation covers six key areas – ethnicity, faith, gender, sexual orientation, age and disability. But you might wish to include other specific groups in your list as well, such as Gypsies and Travellers, asylum seekers, or broader categories, such as economic and social class.

■ When you are presenting your work or your aims to parents or others, make sure you draw attention to the wealth of guidance and legislation that justifies and supports LGBT equalities work (See 'Legislation and guidance' in Chapter 1)

■ Be very careful about language. For example:

☐ References to people's lifestyle in relation to their sexual orientation help to justify the argument that sexual orientation includes some element of choice. This underpins many of the arguments used by the opponents to LGBT equality and is inadvertently perpetuated by well intentioned people.

☐ When talking about LGB relationships with adults, don't confuse sexuality with sexual orientation. Sexual orientation is more specific and an easier term to understand. Sexuality is broader; it refers to the ways in which people experience and express themselves as sexual beings. It's a perfectly good word but some people are concerned about its use in the context of primary classrooms. People sometimes raise absurd objections to LGBT equalities work ('are we going to be including bestiality next?!') and it's worth thinking about how clear use of language can help you avoid such misconceptions.

☐ Avoid using terms like 'alternative families' to describe those that include same sex parents, foster carers etc. This is very excluding. No family is the same – all are different but equally valid.

Aims for an equalities group
Kate

The aims below were developed for Kate's school, but can be adapted for other contexts.

■ The schools aims to work towards achieving a learning community that actively celebrates its own diversity and challenges inequality and injustice

■ The schools aims to develop a range of practical, exciting and fun initiatives about equality and diversity to:

- ensure that all members of the school community, whatever their background, feel accepted, safe and valued

- improve communication between school and parents, guardians and carers regarding equality and diversity and to explore links with relevant outside groups and organisations

- increase awareness of the diversity of family types, backgrounds and experiences in our community

- challenge all forms of discrimination, be it on grounds of ability, socio-economic background, gender, sexual orientation, race or religion

- promote a culture and atmosphere of respect, fairness and justice throughout every aspect of school life

■ The schools aims to feed back to the school and board of governors on equality and diversity issues

■ The schools aims to help develop a school environment, materials and resources, in which discrimination on grounds of religion, class, colour, culture, sexual orientation, gender, origin, domestic background and ability is considered unacceptable.

■ The schools aims to promote equality of opportunity and to identify and eliminate barriers to equality of access, treatment and outcome for everyone in the school

Chapter 7

Planning

Using active learning methods (adapted from Annie's borough-wide resource)
Annie

Active learning methods actively engage children in their own learning processes by enabling them to draw on their own experience. Working collaboratively encourages children to use communication and decision-making skills. Examples include:

Circle time and rounds – facilitate safe, positive environments for discussion and taking turns (more information www.circle-time.co.uk)

Listening exercises – children work in pairs or groups as listeners and speakers and then feed back what they have heard to whole class

Mind maps – children provide words or statements in response to a subject they receive from the teacher, who then facilitates discussion

Case studies – reflection on the actions of a character in a case study; to determine how things could have been done differently

Story telling – using fiction to explore feelings and attitudes

Continuums – a way for children to hear and share a variety of views. After a statement is read out, each child places themselves on the spot which best indicates their views. The teacher then facilitates a discussion based on the positions taken

Puppets – another good distancing technique

Time lines – a useful way of looking at human development

Collages, posters and drawings

ICT – offers effective ways of encouraging active participation

Role-play and drama – allows children to explore their feelings and ideas in a practical situation which simulates real life. Can be done in pairs, small or large groups

Plans for work from nursery to year 6/7
Nikki and Zoe

These plans were designed for input during PSHE (Personal, Social and Health Education) but could also be used elsewhere. They were originally team-taught by Nikki and Zoë together. A 'Responses' section has been added to each plan, showing the responses they received from the children in their school, which serves a largely Muslim population. SEN (Special Educational Needs) and EAL (English as an Additional Language) provision can be adapted according to need. This school uses Makaton (a form of sign language) to aid communication.

Nursery/Reception/Year 1/Year 2	Vocabulary:
Learning Objective: There are lots of different types of families.	Mum, dad, brother, sister, family, home

Teaching Input:

1. Introduce three different families (one with same sex parents, one with a single parent, one with heterosexual parents) using *small world* figures, placing them on three separate coloured circles of paper on table. Share with the children things that the families like to do with each other (be careful not to conform to gender stereotypes) and that they love and care about each other. 2. Set up talk partners. 3. Q – Who is in your family? 4. Choose three children to share who is in their family, using the *small world* figures to show the class.

Plenary:	Follow up:
5. Tell the children that there are lots of different types of families but that what is the same is that they all love and care about each other.	Children use *small world* figures to create different families + photograph for display.

SEN Support:	EAL Support:	Resources:	Other adults:
Use of Makaton, visual figures/objects	talk partners, visual figures/objects, use of	*Small world* figures/objects, table, 3	Support as needed

Responses: '2 mummies?' – giggles

Reception	Vocabulary:
Learning Objective: There are lots of different types of families. Some have two mums and some have two dads.	Penguin, park, zoo, mum, dad, baby, family, egg, nest, zoo keeper

Teaching Input:

1. Introduce the story *And Tango Makes Three*. Q – Who is on the front cover? 2. Read story, support with Powerpoint of images.

Ask Q again – Who is on the front cover? 3. Q – Is there anything that surprised you in the story? Q – What do you think you've learned?

Plenary:	Follow up:
4. Tell the children that there are families with two dads and families with two mums. They do all the same sorts of things that other families do.	Animal family art work for display.

SEN Support:	EAL Support:	Resources:	Other adults:
Use of Makaton, images	talk partners, images, use of Makaton	2 adult penguins, 1 baby penguin, Powerpoint, *And Tango Makes Three*	Support as needed

Responses:
Who is on the front cover? – mummy, daddy and baby penguin (before reading the story)
Who is on the front cover? – baby penguin and his two daddies (after reading the story)

Years 1 and 2	Vocabulary:
Learning Objective: Families can have two mums or two dads. Understand that there are lots of different types of families and we must respect differences.	Mum, dad, brother, sister, step-, single-parent, foster, adopted, grandparents, family

Teaching Input:

1. Q – What makes a family? 2. Discuss front cover of book – *Molly's Family*. Q – Who is on the front cover? 3. As story is read, draw Molly's family on flip chart. 4. Refer back to front cover. Q – Who is on the front cover? 5. Q – Who is in their family? 6. Children draw a picture of who is in their family.

Plenary:	Follow up:
7. Share similarities and differences between families of children in the class. Compare with Molly's family. Say that there are lots of different types of family. There is no 'best' family. We must respect all families. What they have in common is that they love and care for each other.	Visit the family display and find a family that is the same as/different from theirs

SEN Support:	EAL Support:	Resources:	Other adults:
Use of Makaton, pictures, vocabulary check	talk partners, vocabulary check, pictures, use of Makaton	Molly's Family book, worksheet, pencils, colours, flipchart, pens	Support as needed

Responses:
Who is on the front cover? – Molly and her two mummies. Why was Molly sad? – the boy was saying she couldn't have two mummies.

Why did Molly leave her picture at home? – because she didn't want anyone to make fun of her.
What is the 'best' family? – Molly's family, two mummies, everyone's!

Years 3 and 4	Vocabulary:
Learning Objective: To know the correct use of the words *gay* and *lesbian*.	Gay, lesbian, alternative fairy tale, king, queen, princess, prince

Teaching Input:

1. Introduce *King and King* – author, illustrator, front cover. 2. What do you think the story is about? What genre is it? How do fairy tales usually end? 3. Read story. 4. What did you like about the story? Why? What didn't you like about the story? Why? 5. Establish that the correct use of the word 'gay' is to describe a man who loves another man and that the correct use of the word 'lesbian' (or 'gay') is to describe a woman who loves another woman. 6. Show *King and King and Family* and explain that some of the work done in the rest of the school is about celebrating family diversity. 7. Show the 'Introduction' and 'Gay and Lesbian Parents' sections of the *That's a Family* DVD. 6. Invite comments and questions from the children.

Plenary:	Follow up:
Inform the children that when you use the words 'gay' and 'lesbian' incorrectly or to upset someone else this is against our school rules. It is recorded like racist comments are. Your religion might tell you that it is wrong to be gay or lesbian but there are people who are and they should be respected like any other person. 'It's okay to be different!'	Comic strip or storyboard an alternative fairy tale that might include two men or two women who fall in love.

SEN Support:	EAL Support:	Resources:	Other adults:
Adult support	Key vocabulary at the beginning	That's a Family DVD	Support as needed
Pictures in story	Pictures in story	King and King book	
DVD	DVD		

Responses:

'It's haram [forbidden] in my religion to be gay or lesbian'. Response: some Muslims believe that and that's ok, but we must be careful what we say about this in front of others who may have two mums or dads, and we mustn't disrespect someone because they are gay or lesbian.

'My mummy won't like me talking about this'. Response: please ask your mum to come and talk to me: we'd be happy to talk about what we're doing.

Years 5, 6 and 7	Vocabulary:
Learning Objective: What we mean by homophobia and why it is unacceptable.	gay, lesbian, homophobia, homophobic bullying, straight, guy, bloke, civil rights, politician, American terms e.g. Superbowl, Thanksgiving

Teaching Input:

1. Remind the children of the families display on Celebrating Family Diversity. Q – What is the message we're putting across? – all families different but equal.

2. Introduce *Totally Joe* book, discuss American terms. Read chapter 'B is for Boy'. Q's – What is Joe saying? Why is he different? Establish that he is or could be gay. Define words – gay, lesbian. Highlight words that are unacceptable to use as insults e.g. faggot/girl. 3. Elicit famous people who are gay or lesbian, using Powerpoint for support (see resources on the LGBT History Month website at http://lgbthistorymonth.org.uk). 4. Tell the story of Harvey Milk (Powerpoint). 5. We learn by asking questions – children in mixed ability groups develop questions. 6. Groups to feed back top two questions for discussion. 7. Tell the children that some nasty things happen to Joe in *Totally Joe* but he's ok because his friends, family and teachers support him.

Plenary:	
8. Q -What is homophobia? Q – Why is it unacceptable? Q – What can we do about it?	**Follow up:** Plan a song/rap/poem

SEN Support:	EAL Support:	Resources:	Other adults:
adult support, able writers to scribe questions	talk partners, vocabulary check, images, question words	large sheets of paper, pens, Powerpoint, smartboard, Totally Joe and Harvey Milk books, whiteboard	support as needed

Responses:

A Muslim boy asked to go to the toilet during this session and then stayed out of the class. He said that saying the word 'gay' would be worse for him than sticking a hot metal poker in his mouth. However, he understood that we just wanted to make sure that children at our school wouldn't make fun of someone just because they were gay or lesbian, and said that if there was a gay boy in his class he would leave him alone, 'that's his business'.

Labels and symbols
Kate

Suitable for upper Key Stage 2; Allow 30 minutes, plus a further 20 minutes for the art activity.

We should be talking about difference, not just saying we will deal with all the bits that make us similar and then we will appreciate each other more. I've always felt no, we should talk about the bits that make us different because they are the interesting, exciting bits. (Miles)

This lesson was initially developed as part of the Holocaust Memorial Project work with our art club (see Chapter 3) and has since been used each year as part of a Year 6 unit of work about the Second World War. Other lessons included what happened to minority groups in Nazi Germany, and how prejudice built up: from name calling and isolating groups to ultimately killing them. The Imperial War Museum has produced an excellent pack with lesson plans about prejudice. Alongside this unit, children worked in PHSCE and literacy (focusing on poetry) to understand what bullying is, and to explore the roles of the perpetrator, victim and bystander. It is a challenging lesson, but one that can make real changes to attitudes. The signs and symbols used for the lesson follow on page 102: these can be adapted to suit local circumstances. It can be useful to use the colloquial terms of endearment and abuse used by and for people in your local area.

Preparation: one envelope per table containing terms and symbols representing religious and social groups. Some are descriptive (e.g. disabled symbol, Muslim, lesbian), some are used to offend or discriminate against groups (e.g. yellow star used by Nazis to label Jews, words like Paki, spakka), terms 'reclaimed' by groups (e.g. pink triangle originally used by Nazis to label gays, now a gay emblem used by gays and lesbians).

1. Each table is given an envelope containing signs and symbols and a sheet of paper. Ask the children to fold the paper in two and label one half 'good' and the other half 'bad'. The children sort the names and symbols into the two columns, having been assured there is no right or wrong way to do it. Listen in to the discussion as they complete the task and help children out with symbols they don't recognise.

2. Discuss their sorting, especially where there are differences at or between the tables – the symbols and names for gay

and lesbian seem to be the most contentious.

3. Ask the children to do a new 'sort', this time as if they were Nazis. Note what they leave in the 'good' column (probably just 'Christian' and 'white').

4. Explain that we think we are much more tolerant these days – and ask them to sort, this time as our society in general would do, not according to their personal opinions (in the classes I have taught, this leaves the affectionate slang term for local residents, 'Christian' and 'white' on the 'good' side). Tease out in discussion that these labels represent majority groups.

5. Ask children how .... (name someone who has Pakistani parents) would feel if someone called them Paki. How would .... (name someone who is white, but with a dark complexion) feel if they were called Paki? How would ....(the first person named) feel if they overheard the second name calling?

6. How would .... (an adult) feel if someone called them gay or lesbian? Carry on a similar discussion as for racist abuse. This is a powerful opportunity to bring in personal experience of homophobic name calling, especially if the victim is someone the children know personally. Extend the discussion so the children begin to consider the wider impact – the effect on children with gay relatives, or who are not gay but don't fit gender norms etc. You may need to reassure children who revealed homophobic attitudes in the first exercise that you understand their disgust and horror because it is horrible when these terms are used abusively.

In my experience this leads to many children wanting to share their own experiences – of family members who are gay and of how they have been treated, or that the children in the class who don't conform to gender norms feel they are at times marginalised.

7. Explain how some names and symbols are adopted by the group they are used against, and the effect this has (e.g. the term 'queer' and the pink triangle).

8. Follow up with children choosing labels or symbols from their pack to draw, colour, make beautiful. This is a chance for them to relax and continue the discussion informally.

Obese	Gay	Paki	Lesbian	Spakka	Charva	Muslim
Gypsy	Terrorist	Fat	Disabled	White	Jew	Cripple
Black	Asian	Chinky	Nigger			

Alternative fairy tales
Laura

This scheme of work on alternative traditional tales fits into the Year 3 National Literacy Strategy unit on Narrative Themes. It focuses on Text Level Objective 9 (Spring term): *To write a story plan for own myth, fable or traditional tale, using story theme from reading but substituting different characters or changing the setting.*

The lesson plan reads horizontally. You need to begin on the left hand side and move all the way across to the plenary section before moving down. Some of the lessons took longer than an hour, or were spread across different parts of the day. The children who had low literacy skills were given a writing frame for describing their alternative Cinderella characters.

I chose to use the story of Cinderella, but others can be used. I got my whole class to work on the story so that we were all adapting the same parts of it at the same time. If I did it again, I would probably establish a setting for all the children to use so they could to concentrate more on the character they were adapting. I wanted the children to take up LGBT characters if they

wished, so I included LGBT identity alongside other possible ways of changing the identities of their characters – for example, in terms of skin colour, culture, disability, gender or the way in which the characters perform their gender. And I would narrow this down to only skin colour and gender/sexuality unless I had read texts with the children that dealt positively with other equalities areas.

Towards the end of the first week, I performed the story for my class from the perspective of a lesbian Cinderella character. This provided an engaging and concrete starting point for the children to discuss the similarities and differences between my story and the traditional story they had read earlier. They made puppets of their own alternative Cinderella characters and used these to act out possible alternative stories in groups. Before they wrote their stories, their alternative Cinderella puppets introduced themselves to each other.

Many of the children across the whole unit of work were reluctant to explore different identities for fairytale characters. Early in the week we looked at ways in which Elizabeth from *The Paper Bag Princess* differed from Cinderella. Although the children appeared to disapprove of Cinderella's passivity, many found it difficult to be Elizabeth and advise Cinderella on fashion and marriage. They were worried that if they told Cinderella that she does not have to wear uncomfortable ball dresses and glass slippers, and that she should choose her husband carefully, Prince Charming might reject her.

When we read *King and King* children had questions on the legality of gay marriage and a few reacted very negatively to the idea that lesbians could get married. Despite long discussions with the children about the Princes being gay and getting married, some of them continued to talk about Prince Bertie wanting to marry a Princess. When it came to making the puppets, some children needed persuading to alter their own Cinderella characters. Many simply wanted to replicate the character of the traditional Cinderella. Next time I might have children pick a card with a suggestion about how their character could be different and ask them to use this in their story.

From the lesson plan: terms and abbreviations

IWB = Interactive Whiteboard

TP – talk partners

synonyms 'splat'- a game where the teacher places words around the classroom and children compete to go and touch (or 'splat') the word that is a synonym to the word displayed on the board

WILF (What I'm Looking For) is a strategy for keeping learning objectives in children's minds and focusing on them in discussion

2 stars and a wish – two aspects of the work that have met the WILF and one aspect that needs to be improved.

Zone of Proximity – put a picture of a character in the middle of a sheet of paper then draw two rings around the picture so that the page is in three sections. Give the children a list of nouns and adjectives on post-it notes to place around the character. The words they think apply most to the character go nearest to the character in the middle of the page, those they think totally irrelevant go on the outside. The children then have to justify where they have placed the words, using evidence from the text. They can try to persuade each other to move a word.

	Whole Class Shared Session	Guided Session	Independent / Group Activities	Plenary
Mon.	1) Thought shower ingredients for fairy tale – 'once upon a time', 'happily ever after', magic, talking animals, contrasting characters, repeated phrases.	Complete big zone of proximity posters.	1) Talk partners to recap on features.	1) Scribe on IWB as children feed back on features.
	2) Recap on Cinderella story – read extract noting adjectives and connectives (on IWB). Choose children to come to act out whilst extract is read.		2) Children fill in zone of proximity for Cinderella – would the book still be a fairy tale if we moved some of these words?	2) Discuss whether the book would still be a fairy tale if we moved some of these words.
	3) Read Amazing Grace by Mary Hoffman up to part when Grace is told she can't be Peter Pan because she is Black and because she is a girl.		3) Discuss reasons why children in book said those things. Do children agree? Read rest of story – children fill in Zone of Proximity for Grace. Do they like Grace?	3) Ask children to justify where they placed words for Grace and Cinderella – compare the two zones of proximity.
Tues.	1) Read *The Paper Bag Princess* – using paper bag dress and pictures with key vocab words to support children who have SEN and EAL.	Work with individual group(s) as appropriate.	1) One child takes role of Cinderella and mimes certain parts of Cinderella story. children in class give advice to Cinderella as if they were Elizabeth (the Paperbag Princess). The children discuss the advice in pairs first.	1) Discuss main character traits of Elizabeth and Cinderella.
	2) Model writing short letter of advice from Elizabeth to Cinderella.	Blue group to complete task with additional support and writing frame.	2) Children write letters from Elizabeth to Cinderella.	2) Take a child's work – whole class assess against WILF (What I'm Looking For) – 2 stars and a wish.
	3) Play synonyms 'splat'.		3) Put words to describe Elizabeth around the class. Children to choose synonyms from words on tables to go next to words on wall.	3) Discuss answers and consider which are best words to use. Which words are 'wow' words?
Wed.	1) Give children scroll tied with ribbon on which is written a letter from Prince Bertie asking Year 3 for advice – his mother says everyone his age has been married at least twice, he's had to meet lots of princesses but doesn't want to marry them etc.		1) Discuss why Prince Bertie might not want to marry the princesses. What could he do?	1) Read *King and King*.

	Whole Class Shared Session	Guided Session	Independent / Group Activities	Plenary
	2) In TP pairs children thought shower words (adjectives and verbs) to describe Bertie and what he likes doing – give 2 mins to come up with words.	Use thesauruses with yellow group to generate good vocabulary.	2). Scribe suggestions around picture of Bertie on A3 sheet. Red group have thesauruses so they can help us to improve vocabulary.	2) Children tell TPs what Prince Bertie is like.
	3) Model writing lonely hearts ad from Bertie. Remind children about varying sentence structure – beginning sentences with adverbs etc.		3) Children write ad from Bertie to other Princes, using adjectives and adverbs. Give blue group sentence starters on table.	3) Share superstar sentences and assess against WILF.
Thurs	1) Explain that we will write a story like Cinderella but we will change it.	Support children who need extra help.	1) Create alternative Cinderella and relay events in story (but obviously altered) to children	1) Children hotseat alternative Cinderella.
	2). Discuss ways in which children can change Cinderella's character.		2) Model making alternative Cinderella puppet, then children make their own puppets.	
Fri.	1) Continue making puppets.	Support children in explaining and justifying choices in story plan.	1) When finished, children introduce the alternative Cinderellas they have created to each other, saying where they have come from, where they live, what their name is, what their story is etc.	
	2) Model planning alternative Cinderella tale on simple planning sheet.		2) Children plan own stories in words or pictures or both.	2) Within groups, children hotseat one group member to ask questions about alternative story.

Plans for key stages 1 and 2
Andrew

These lesson plans are included in two resources which Andrew wrote as part of his No Outsiders *project work: a resource on challenging homophobia for early years and one on emotional literacy for Key Stage 2 (these last two plans are part of 'Emotional literacy: a scheme of work for the primary school' written by Andrew Moffat and published by Incentive Plus; they are reproduced here with permission). Although written for specific year groups, they can be adapted to others. They can be linked to SEAL, emotional literacy work and the Healthy Schools programme. They use a range of children's books, some of which are from the* No Outsiders *book collection.*

Year 2

Knowledge, understanding and skills (SEAL)	Activities	Resources
New beginnings I know what I have to do make the classroom and school a safe and fair place for everyone, and I know it is not OK for some people to make it unsafe or unfair for others.	**Read *King and King*.** **Discussion**: What happens in this story? Why do you think the Prince doesn't want to marry any of the Princesses his mother brings to him? Is he gay? What does gay mean? Do you think if he tried he could be happy marrying a princess? Should he at least try to fall in love with a princess? Is that what the Queen wants? Or does she want him to be happy?	*King and King* by Linda de Haan and Stern Nijland
Say no to bullying I can tell you what bullying is.	**Role play**: Show the children cards portraying a selection of people. Explain we are going to set up a marriage scene for the prince and prince. Every person on the cards is at the wedding. All we have to do is identify what their role is and place them in the scene. Begin by placing a table at the top of the scene. Now ask the first child to choose one of the Princes from the pile of cards. The next child should choose his partner. Continue in the round, asking children to develop the scene by adding people from the range of cards and adding them to the picture, saying who they are. You might want odd roles such as registrar, best man (for both grooms), family members, photographer, witness etc	People cards (I use cut-outs of people from clothes catalogues. Be sure there is a good male and female, disability and ethnic mix)

Knowledge, understanding and skills (SEAL)	Activities	Resources
	Plenary: Are there any other fairy tales where a Prince marries a Prince and they live happily ever after? Why not? Could a Princess marry a Princess and live happily ever after? Of course! Note: if someone brings up the question of how they can have children, open it out to the group. Could they adopt? Maybe one of the princes already has a child. Note: There is a sequel book, King and King and Family, where the two kings adopt a little girl. Do the King and King look unhappy about being gay? Is anyone calling them names or making them feel unwelcome? Of course not. Would we call them names if they were in our class? Might be bullied at school? What would you do if you saw someone calling them names? Is our class safe for everyone? It doesn't matter if someone is gay, does it?	

Year 2

Knowledge, understanding and skills (SEAL)	Activities	Resources
Relationships: I know the people who are important to me. I can tell when I feel cared for. I can tell when I love or care for someone. I understand that if someone leaves me they might still love me. I understand that people have to make hard choices and sometimes they have no choice.	***Read Mr Seahorse*** **Discussion**: What happens in the story? What is the seahorse doing during the story? Who does he meet along the way who is also looking after babies? In what different ways are the Daddy fishes looking after their babies? What does Mr Seahorse say to the baby seahorse who tries to get back in to the pouch? Why does he say that? Do you think that's a hard choice for Mr Seahorse to make? How do we know that Mr Seahorse loves his babies very much? **Role play**: Show the children a bag of marbles tied at the top. Explain that we are going to pretend that these are Mr Seahorse's babies. Choose someone to be Mr Seahorse and give the bag to him (*Note: it really should be a boy, as we are making the point that men can look after babies and bring up children*). Now put the children into pairs and ask them to decide what sea animals they are going to be, and to decide upon an action that they can do when they speak. Once everyone is ready, ask Mr Seahorse to swim to the pairs in the circle and say 'Hello'. The children will then say, 'Hello, Mr Seahorse. We are _____' and perform their action. Mr Seahorse will then say 'Nice to meet you, I'm looking after my babies' and swim back to the centre of the circle before approaching a different pair. At the end of the role play ask Mr Seahorse to set his children free. He should gently tip out the marbles and watch them swim away	*Mr Seahorse* by Eric Carle Bag of marbles

Knowledge, understanding and skills (SEAL)	Activities	Resources
	Plenary: Do you think the story is based on truth? Do male seahorses look after their young? (They do). Mr Seahorse meets lots of male fish in the story who are also looking after their young. Do you think it's right that they do that? Are men good at looking after children? Are women better? Does it matter who brings up children? Are there good things about both men and women bringing up children? *Note: You could ask the class who brings up the children – who lives with Mum, with Dad, with Nan or Grandad, with two Dads or Mums, with Aunty, etc to demonstrate that there is not one model that fits all and we all live in different families and that's okay.* What do you think is the most important thing in a family – love? The children could make a card for the people in their home they love.	

Year 3/4 Emotional Literacy: Happy and Sad (using One dad two dads brown dad blue dads by Johnny Valentine and a piece of paper for each child)

Learning Intention	Activities
To increase empathy for others and awareness of how personal feelings and behaviours can impact upon others. To understand what might make a person feel sad, and what it feels like to be happy.	Recap words 'Happy' and 'Sad'. What situations can make a person happy and sad? **Read**: *One dad two dads brown dad blue dads* **Discussion**: What is this book about? Does it make sense? What do you think is the message the author is trying to tell us? That it doesn't matter what colour skin you have, or who you live with, or the different ways you live your life, we are all different and that's ok. Look at the page 'If they hug you too hard does the colour rub off?' What does that mean? Does it? Is the child telling us the story happy to have two blue dads? Why is he happy? *Note: Here is a great opportunity to talk about gay parents. Be sensitive to the possibility that there may be children in your class who have gay parents. Now might be a good time to celebrate diversity in our class; we are all different and isn't that great! You also might like to reinforce the school rules about name calling and bullying. Saying something or someone is 'gay' as a put-down is not acceptable in our class. It's like teasing someone because they have blue eyes!* **Role play**: The aim is to recognise how we are all different and accept that there is no single model we are all striving to be. Ask the children to think of one statement about themselves which they think makes them different to everyone else. You could focus on hair or skin colour, or hobbies, or home situations. It is important that the children choose what they wish to share and focus on. We shouldn't tell anyone how they are different; the aim is to get everyone to identify one way for themselves. When everyone has written down their statement, put all the pieces of paper in a hat and shake it up. Now say we are going to celebrate how diverse our class is (you might want to define diversity). Ask the children, one at a time, to pick a statement out of the hat and read it out aloud. Discourage the children from guessing who made what statement. Instead, celebrate how many different people from different backgrounds we have in our class. You could print out the statements and make a display.

Learning Intention	Activities
	Activity: Make a poster celebrating diversity in our class.
	Plenary: What a great class this is! So many different people and so much experience in one room! Is anyone better than anyone else? Is it better to be one way than another? We should be happy to be who we are and proud of who we are and where we come from. We are all special.

Year 5/6 Emotional Literacy: Proud and Ashamed (using *William's Doll* by Charlotte Zolotow)

Learning Intention	Activities
To increase empathy for others and awareness of how personal feelings and behaviours can impact upon others. To understand what makes a person feel proud and why someone may feel ashamed.	Discuss the words 'proud' and 'ashamed'. Give examples of times when we might feel proud and ashamed.
	Read: *William's Doll*
	Discussion: What is this story about? What are the central themes to the story? Why do you think William's Dad buys William a basketball and a train set? Did playing with these toys make William happy? Do you think William's Dad wants William to be happy? Who changes the situation in the story? Why do you think Grandma buys William a doll? Do you think she was right to do that? What is the argument she uses at the end of the story? Look again at the last page. What do you think about what she says? Do girls and boys play with different toys in real life? What toys do you think girls play with? What toys do you think boys play with? Why do you think that is? Are there exceptions? Do boys get laughed at for playing with dolls? Do girls get laughed at for playing with train sets or playing football? Is it right that this happens? Do you think we should change this? How do we change it?
	Role play/Activity: There are a couple of things you could do for a role play depending on your school situation:
	■ If you are a primary school with a Reception class, arrange to take your class down to Reception to role play with the children there. But first discuss what each child in your class might want to play with. Do we want all the boys in Reception to think boys only play football or building bricks? Similarly do we want to teach our Reception children that girls only play dressing up or with dolls? The boys in your class should play with things they would normally expect girls to play with, and the girls with things they would normally expect boys to play with. Reinforce how vital it is that we are role models. The little children will take from our lead. If we look embarrassed, they will pick up on it. It's only for 15 minutes!
	■ In pairs role play the argument between Gran and Dad about buying William a doll. Think about the worries that dad might have and his reasons for arguing against the doll. Share some of the role plays.
	Plenary:
	■ It may be that the children in Reception are more enlightened than us and feel they can play with whatever they want. Were the boys playing with 'boy things'? How interesting! So at what point do boys begin to realise they 'shouldn't' play with dolls or dress up? Did the boys in Reception stop what they were doing and gravitate to the older boys, and the girls gravitate to older girls? How did it feel to be a role model? Did any Reception children argue you shouldn't be playing with these toys because you were a boy or a girl? What did you say?

Exploring gender and identity in the primary classroom
Jay

These activities could be carried out as a single session or spread over several. Of course you don't have to be trans to do this lesson. And it may be that as a teacher you might not want to offer pupils your self-portrait, but it might be an opportunity to express various, possibly contradictory parts of your gendered self. For example, you may enjoy wearing dresses, but also play football. Or you may see yourself as gender neutral.

For myself, introducing myself as a trans man was crucial to the success of the lesson, as this allowed the pupils to see a 'real' trans man. It also gave them an opportunity to ask questions and to acquire some empathy about some of the decisions and experiences I have faced in my life.

Young people tend to be concerned about whether I maintained my friendships, or how my family responded to my being trans, and whether that was hard for me. It was encouraging, I feel, to ensure them that coming out as trans does not necessarily mean you will lose all your friendships.

The children might ask questions about the various medical interventions and surgical options that are possible. Whilst not avoiding these questions, I feel it's important to stress that surgery and medical intervention isn't an essential part of being trans, though it's an option that is available; that there are lots of different choices people can make.

Activity	Teaching points
INTRODUCTION Who am I? I'm an Artist – asking the question 'who am I?' artists ask. When we do art, we also can ask some of these questions, such as Today we are all going to ask ourselves that question and produce some self-portraits. 'who am I?'	The starting point here is about what artists do and what kinds of questions artists ask. When we do art, we also can ask some of these questions, such as 'who am I'

INTRODUCING GENDER
(Key terms: gender; boy/girl; male/female; gender identity)
 	
Map out responses to some of the following questions:
 	
■ What is gender? – being a girl or a boy; explain that we all have a gender
■ How do you know someone is a boy or a girl?
 	
SHOW PICTURE OF BABY
■ What happens when you are born?
  You are given a birth certificate
  You are assigned a gender based on your body
■ What happens then?
  You develop your gender identity by what you like to wear, what you like to do; how you choose to express who you are
 	
SHOW PICTURE OF YOUNG PEOPLE
■ What do boys look like?
■ What do girls look like?
■ HOW DO WE KNOW?
 	
■ What do boys wear?
■ What do girls wear?
■ HOW DO WE KNOW?
 	
SHOW PICTURE OF TOYS
■ What do boys like to do?
■ What do girls like to do?
■ HOW DO WE KNOW?
	The children might refer to genitals as part of the discussion around defining gender and this is okay. A good response would be to respond using the terms for them in accordance with school policy. Many schools make a point of using accurate terms from an early age.
	
	The children may already be exploring male-female differences in sex and relationships education. If so, this may prove useful as knowledge about secondary sex characteristics and hormones such as oestrogen and testosterone might also arise.
	
	What is being explored here is the way in which we 'read' gender – as children and as adults – from culturally determined signals.
	
	These questions are intended to be provocative. They are not intended to reinforce gender stereotypes! In fact, the word 'stereotype' may come up for discussion.
	
	This questioning activity also establishes that not everyone in the class might agree on these gendered behaviours, showing that what it means to be a boy or a girl is not a fixed idea.

SHOW PICTURE OF FAMILIES/ROLES/JOBS/HOBBIES ■ How do boys act? ■How do girls act? ■HOW DO WE KNOW ■ What about grown ups? What do they do? ■ How do men act? ■ How do women act? ■ HOW DO WE KNOW?	

EXPLORING GENDERED BEHAVIOUR
(Key terms: girlish/boyish; feminine/masculine; gender stereotype)
SHOW PICTURES OF GIRLS DOING BOYISH THINGS AND VICE VERSA
 	
■ Are some boys more boyish than others?
■ Are some girls more girlish than others?
■ Can you be a girl and do boyish things?
  Eg. Can girls play football?
■ Can you be a boy and do girlish things?
  Eg. Can boys do ballet?
 	
Our gender is an important part of who we are. But it may sometimes also get in the way if people have fixed ideas about which gender does what.
	The point here is not to invite pupils to identify particularly girlish boys or boyish girls, but to explore the ways in which assigning gender to certain behaviours may be unhelpful to some (or all!) people.
	
	It is important to underline the idea that it's possible and (importantly) it's *okay* for 'girls' to enjoy doing 'boyish' things and for 'boys' to enjoy doing 'girlish' things.

MULTI-MEDIA SELF-PORTRAIT Each pupil has a large sheet of paper entitled 'Who am I?' Using available resources (e.g. photography, computer image manipulation, drawing, painting, collage, writing etc) and with support as appropriate, each pupil creates their own multi-media self-portrait. Both boys and girls include the following statements in their self-portrait. ■ I have... (what you look like) ■ I like playing with... ■ I like wearing ... ■ I want to be... ■ Some of the girlish things I like doing are... ■ Some of the boyish things I like doing are... ■ When I was born I was assigned ..... at birth (to be completed by each pupil)	The aim of this exercise is to allow individuals to express their gendered self. It maybe that there are aspects of themselves that they might see as girlish and aspects of themselves that they might see as boyish (or even that other people might see them as this). An individual may feel they are more boyish or more girlish one way or the other and that also is okay. The point here is to undo gender stereotypes, but it's equally fine if some of the girls don't identify any boyish things they like to do and some of the boys don't identify any girlish things: the important thing is to have the freedom to choose. Some discussion that might come out of this may concern the extent to which a person can choose. You might discuss how our choices are influenced by a market-driven Western European society (particularly concerning toy choices) and how direct and indirect experiences of bullying might

When the portraits are completed, exhibit them in the classroom, give everyone time to look at them and discuss interesting points re breaking gender stereotypes.

BREAKING GENDER BOUNDARIES

(Key terms: transgendered; trans man; trans woman; transvestite/cross dresser; gender specific; gender variant)

- Can you be a girl and do boyish things? Examples?
- Can you be a boy and do girlish things? Examples?
- What about cross dressing?
- What if you don't like being female/ male?
- Can someone who is assigned female at birth become a boy or a man?

Introduce the terms transgendered, trans man, trans woman, gender specific; gender variant

Any questions?

influence our choices. (This might in particular be around 'boys' who like to do 'girlish' things.)

When discussion ensues around (for instance) being a 'boy' and enjoying doing 'girlish' things, the pupils may raise some interesting words such as transvestite or transsexual, as these words abound in the mainstream media and they may well have heard them. For instance, the case of Thomas Beattie, the pregnant man, has been a very popular story.

As with words around genitalia, it's important to ensure that you have picked up these words and offered them up for discussion.

The fact is that some people cross dress, and some people might change their bodies from the sex that they were assigned at birth. It is important that the teacher's response is 'That's okay'.

The opportunity here is to deepen understanding, to ensure pupils understand that there is nothing wrong with being transgendered.

Overview of sequence of lessons for years 5 and 6
Annie

This excerpt from Annie's borough-wide resource provides an overview of a sequence of lesson plans for Years 5 and 6. A questionnaire related to Year 6, lesson 2 is also included. The questionnaire could be used within training and awareness-raising for teaching and non-teaching staff, governors and parents.

Year group	Objective	Brief description of activity
Year 5 Lesson 1	To be able to identify positive personal qualities and aspects of personal identity.	Pupils draw and write about themselves.
Year 5 Lesson 2	To understand that people are different and that these differences can be celebrated.	Pupils attribute positive adjectives to other members of the class.
Year 5 Lesson 3	To understand the term 'prejudice' in terms of relationships.	Using a Venn diagram, pupils sort photographs of a range of different couples into sections; 'may experience prejudice', 'unlikely to experience prejudice' and 'may be a positive relationship'.
	To understand that 'prejudice' affects people in a negative way.	
Year 5 Lesson 4	To be able to show respect for diversity in society, including lesbian, gay and bisexual relationships.	Pupils design an emblem/motif which says: 'We are all special and we are all different.'
Year 6 Lesson 1	To understand a possible consequence of gender stereotyping and homophobic bullying.	Pupils act as experts to investigate a bullying problem.
Year 6 Lesson 2	To know key facts about the law and homophobia.	Pupils respond to a questionnaire to develop knowledge about LGB identities and the law.
	To know key facts about the law, civil liberties and lesbian, gay and bisexual relationships.	
Year 6 Lesson 3	To be able to think of strategies to challenge homophobic bullying.	Pupils act as experts to solve the bullying problem investigated in lesson 1.
	To develop social negotiation skills.	

'True/False' questionnaire about LGB issues
Annie

1. It is not possible for gay/lesbian/bisexual couples to get married.

   Answer. False, although it is not called marriage. *The Civil Partnership Act 2004 came into operation on 5 December 2005 and enables same-sex couples to register as civil partners. For more information* see: http://www.gro.gov.uk/gro/content/civilpartnerships/

2. It is illegal for teachers to talk about gay relationships in the classroom

   Answer: False

3. There is no such thing as a homophobic hate crime in British Law

   Answer: False

4. In British Law there is no legal protection for a lesbian or a gay man who is sacked from their job because they are gay/lesbian.

   Answer: False

5. How many countries in Western Europe allow legally binding same sex partnerships?

   (Answer underlined):   None   2   6   <u>10+</u>

6. What percentage of gay men in this country have experienced homophobic verbal abuse?

   (Answer underlined):   16%   22%   <u>68%</u>   98%

7. What percent of gay men in this country who have experienced homophobic abuse have reported it to the police?

   (Answer underlined):   16%   <u>18%</u>   49%   63%

PGCE Primary English
Katherine

This plan could be used by teacher-training tutors as well as for professional development in schools, and might be spread over several sessions to allow for deeper exploration. The reference to QTS (Qualified Teacher Status) standards will be of value to UK-based class teachers with trainees placed in their classrooms.

Purpose – To look at texts used by the *No Outsiders* project. Trainees will be introduced to government policy and invited to question their personal beliefs (prejudices?) and perhaps to readjust their approaches to equality within the classroom.

Key Questions	What is gender? Is it fixed? How should/could we promote gender equality within our classrooms? Why should this be taught at primary school (schools as ideally placed, teacher responsibility)? How will the texts help (especially considering the idea that children learn through narrative)? What does it feel like to be an insider or outsider? What is identity and what is my identity? What is gender normative/heteronormative behaviour? Is the world constantly divided into male or female? Are those boundaries fluid? Visit gender stereotypes relating to role, job, behaviour and ways of thinking. Can anyone be a ballet dancer? How could we deal with homophobic behaviour in schools using these books? Link to media attention. What do the students feel about the project books? Feedback.
Content	1. Establish working environment for the session: whatever we say stays in the room. Everyone does their best to be open minded. Ideas expressed by other group members are to be treated with sensitivity and respect. If someone doesn't feel comfortable, they should feel free to say so. Tolerance, understanding and respect are the basis for discussion.
	2. Ask trainees to consider their own identity. What makes them who they are? Give five minutes to jot ideas down. Does anyone identify themselves by gender? Each of us has our own identity and gender and each one of us should feel included.
	3. Link to idea of *No Outsiders*. Introduce project and Desmond Tutu's view that '*Everyone is an insider, there are no outsiders – whatever their beliefs, whatever their colour, gender or sexuality*' (February 2004).

Play insider/outsider game. In teams of 3, trainees to make a list of all teams they can think of.

When did you feel part of a team? When did you feel excluded? Can you name a time when you excluded someone? Can you name a time when you've made an effort to include someone?

Discuss in groups and possibly tableau. How have those occasions made you feel? How would it feel if you were a child?

4. Legal Standpoint- see Stonewall document *Education for All* 2005. Teachers are free to discuss homophobia with their students in the classroom. Primary schools are ideally placed to challenge stereotypes, as these significantly influence the development of values and attitudes in young children.

5. Discussion task. In small groups around the room- 'what is gender?' ten minutes for ideas and 5 to feed back to the rest of the group. (Gender is not something you are or have but is something that you do).

6. Scribble paper divided into male/female. 1 minute to jot down as many stereotypes as can be thought of for roles, jobs, behaviours, images, ways of thinking. How could we challenge these? Share *Sissy Duckling* book.

7. Family task- what makes a family? How would you feel if, when talking about family at school, your family wasn't represented? Link to *If I had a 100 mummies'* and *And Tango Makes Three* books

8. *No Outsiders* books- trainees to look at a selection of the project books to gain knowledge of what is available to them. Using the books, trainees make a display – e.g. create a plan for an inclusion week centred on one of the books, a lesson to do with a book or a poster advocating use of books in primary school.

9. Feedback at end of session- reactions to books and project.

Selected relevant QTS Standards

Q1 Have high expectations of children and young people including a commitment to ensuring that each can achieve their full educational potential and to establishing fair, respectful, trusting, supportive and constructive relationships with them.

Q2 Demonstrate the positive values, attitudes and behaviour they expect from children and young people.

Q3 (a) Be aware of the professional duties of teachers and the statutory framework within which they work.

(b) Be aware of the policies and practices of the workplace and share in collective responsibility for their implementation.

Q8 Have a creative and constructively critical approach towards innovation, being prepared to adapt their practice where benefits and improvements are identified.

Q15 Know and understand the relevant statutory and non-statutory curricula and frameworks, including those provided through the National Strategies, for their subjects/curriculum areas, and other relevant initiatives applicable to the age and ability range for which they are trained.

Q18 Understand how children and young people develop and that the progress and well-being of learners are affected by a range of developmental, social, religious, ethnic, cultural and linguistic influences.

Q19 Know how to make effective personalised provision for those they teach, including those for whom English is an additional language or who have special educational needs or disabilities, and how to take practical account of diversity and promote equality and inclusion in their teaching.

Q21 (a) Be aware of the current legal requirements, national policies and guidance on the safeguarding and promotion of the well-being of children and young people.

(b) Know how to identify and support children and young people whose progress, development or well-being is affected by changes or difficulties in their personal circumstances, and when to refer them to colleagues for specialist support.

Q30 Establish a purposeful and safe learning environment conducive to learning and identify opportunities for learners to learn in out-of-school contexts.

Chapter 8

Information and Resources

No Outsiders Project Resources

ABC: A family alphabet book by Bobbie Combs

And Tango Makes Three by Peter Parnell and Justin Richardson

Are You a Boy or a Girl? (DVD story board version) by Karleen Pendleton Jimenez

Asha's Mums by Rosamund Elwin, Michele Paulse and Dawn Lee

The Daddy Machine by Johnny Valentine and Lynette Schmidt

Daddy's Roommate by Michael Willhoite

The Harvey Milk Story by Kari Krakow and David Gardner

Heather Has Two Mommies by Leslea Newman and Diana Souza

Inventing Elliot by Graham Gardner

If I Had 100 Mummies by Vanda Carter

King and King by Linda De Haan and Stern Nijland

King and King and Family by Linda De Haan and Stern Nijland

Molly's Family by Nancy Garden and Sharon Wooding

Mummy Never Told Me by Babette Cole

Oliver Button Is a Sissy by Tomie de Paola

One Dad, Two Dads, Brown Dad, Blue Dad by Johnny Valentine and Melody Sarecky

Priscilla and the Pink Planet by Nathaniel Hobbie and Jocelyn Hobbie

Something Else by Kathryn Cave and Chris Riddell

Spacegirl Pukes by Katy Watson and Vanda Carter

That's a Family (video) GroundSpark Productions, directed by Debra Chasnoff

The Family Book by Todd Parr

The Princesses Have a Ball by Teresa Bateman and Lynne Cravath

The Sissy Duckling by Harvey Fierstein and Henry Cole

Totally Joe by James Howe

Two Weeks with the Queen by Morris Gleitzman

We Do: A celebration of gay and lesbian marriage by Gavin Newsom and Amy Rennert

While You Were Sleeping by John Butler

William's Doll by Charlotte Zolotow and William Pene du Bois

Posters:

Real Families Rock created by Out for Our Children and available at http://www.outforourchildren.co.uk

Gender subversion created by CrimethInc. and available at http://www. buyolympia.com/crimethinc/sid=332423730/post.html

Respect for All Families Family Poster created by COLAGE and available at http://www.colage.org/ylap/posters.html

Respect for All Families Group Poster created by COLAGE and available at http://www.colage.org/ylap/posters.html

LGBT Support Groups and Activist Organisations

A Day in Hand (A silent revolution through same-sex hand holding) http://www.adayinhand.com/

Beatbullying
http://www.beatbullying.org/

COLAGE, A national (US-based) movement of children, youth, and adults with one or more lesbian, gay, bisexual, transgender and/or queer (LGBTQ) parent http://www.colage.org/

Families and Friends of Lesbians and Gays (FFLAG) http://www.fflag.org.uk/

Gay, Lesbian and Straight Education Network (GLSEN), US-based http://www.glsen.org/cgi-bin/iowa/all/about/index.html

General Teaching Council for England (GTCE) Code of Conduct and Practice for Registered

Teachers (includes sexual orientation) http://www.gtce.org.uk/documents/publicationpdfs/conduct_code_pccpt1007.pdf

IDAHO (International Day Against Homophobia) 17th May, 2006 http://www.homophobiaday.org/

International Lesbian Gay Association (ILGA) http://www.ilga.org/

LGBT History Month UK (initiated by Schools Out in February 2005) http://www.lgbthistorymonth.org.uk/

National Union of Teachers (NUT) guidance for members on sexual orientation discrimination http://www.teachers.org.uk/story.php?id=3019

Naz Project London (targeted to Black and Minority Ethnic (BME) youth http://www.naz.org.uk/index.html

Newfamilysocial, a UK support group for lesbian and gay adopters http://www.newfamilysocial.co.uk/

Out For Our Children, a group of London lesbian parents producing books and resources that reflect our children's lives and family experiences http://www.outforourchildren.co.uk/

Pink Parents
http://www.pinkparents.org.uk/

Schools Out
http://www.schools-out.org.uk/

Stonewall
http://www.stonewall.org.uk/

Trans and Gender Variance Information, Support and Activism

Gendered Intelligence: understanding gender diversity in creative ways http://www.genderedintelligence.co.uk/

Press for Change: Campaigning for respect and equality for ALL trans people http://www.pfc.org.uk/

Mermaids, a support gropup for non-gender conforming children and teenagers http://www.mermaidsuk.org.uk/

Gender Identity Research and Education Society (GIRES) http://www.gires.org.uk/

Intersex Society of North America www.isna.org

Depend, a support group for spouses, partners, family members and friends of transsexual people http://www.depend.org.uk/

The Transgender Zone – support and information http://www.transgenderzone.com/index.htm

A Place at the Table – training, jobfairs and conferences for organisations http://www.aplaceatthetable.co.uk/

TransBiblio – Bibliography of print, av, and online resources compiled by the University of Illinois at Urbana-Champaign Library http://www.library.illinois.edu/edx/womensstudies/transbiblio.html

Women Make Movies (WMM): transgender and intersex documentaries http://www.nooutsiders. sunderland.ac.uk/trans-gender-queer-activism-support-information/WMM%20Highlights%20 Transgender%20and%20Intersex%20Issues.doc/ view

Gender Spectrum – US, west-coast based support organization http://www.genderspectrum.org/

Religious Support for LGBT people

100Revs: Christian ministers apologise for their lack of welcome to the gay community http://100revs.blogspot.com

Affirmation: a group for gay and lesbian Mormons http://www.affirmation.org

Affirmation: United Methodists for LGBT concerns http://umaffirm.org

Al-Fatiha Foundation, promoting progressive Islamic notions of peace, equality and justice http://www.al-fatiha.org

The Evangelical Fellowship for Lesbian and Gay Christians (EFLGC) http://www.eflgc.org.uk

GALVA: Gay and Lesbian Vaishnava Association http://www.galva108.org

Imaan: for LGBT Muslims and their supporters http://www.imaan.org.uk

The Jewish Gay and Lesbian Group http://www.jglg.org.uk/

LGCM: Lesbian and Gay Christian Movement http://www.lgcm.org.uk

Metropolitan Community Churches – founded within and reaching beyond the LGBT-community http://www.mccchurch.org/AM/Template.cfm?Sec tion=Home

Quest: a group for lesbian and gay Catholics http://questgaycatholic.org.uk/home.asp

Religious Tolerance – Religious groups' policies & beliefs about homosexuality http://www.religioustolerance.org/hom_chur.htm

The Safra Project for lesbian, bisexual and/or transgender women who identify as Muslim religiously and/or culturally http://www.safraproject.org

SARBAT.NET, the website for Lesbian, Gay, Bisexual and Transgendered (LGBT) Sikhs http://www.sarbat.net/

Other Publications from the *No Outsiders* project team

Allan, A, Atkinson, E, Brace, E, DePalma, R and Hemingway, J (2008) Speaking the unspeakable in forbidden places: addressing lesbian, gay, bisexual and transgender equality in the primary school. *Sex Education*, 8(3) 315-328

Atkinson, E (2007) Speaking with small voices: voice, resistance and difference. In Reiss, M, Atkinson, E and DePalma, R (eds) *Marginality and Difference in Education and Beyond* Stoke-on-Trent, Trentham, 15-29

Atkinson, E and DePalma, R (2009) Unbelieving the matrix: Queering consensual heteronormativity. *Gender & Education* 21(1) 17-29

Cullen, F and Sandy, L (2009) Lesbian Cinderella and other stories: Telling tales and researching sexualities equalities in primary school. *Sex Education* 9(2), 141-154

DePalma, R (2009) Leaving Alinsu: towards a transformative community of practice. *Mind, Culture, and Activity* 16(4), pp. 353 – 370

DePalma, R (2009) Sexualities equality in all primary schools: A case for not waiting for ideal conditions. In Koschoreck, J W and Tooms, A A (eds) *Sexuality matters: Paradigms and policies for educational leaders.* Plymouth, Rowman & Littlefield

DePalma, R (in press) Homophobia, transphobia and culture: Deconstructing heteronormativity in English primary schools. *Intercultural Education*

DePalma, R and Atkinson, E (2006) *No Outsiders*: a University-school collaboration to help stamp out homophobia. *Snapshots: The Specialist Schools and Academies Trust Journal of Innovation in Education, Primary Edition* 3 (3) 11-13

DePalma, R and Atkinson, E (2007) Exploring gender identity; queering heteronormativity. *International Journal of Equity and Innovation in Early Childhood*, 5(2) 64-82

DePalma, R and Atkinson, E (eds) (2009) *Interrogating heteronormativity in primary schools: The work of the No Outsiders Project*. Stoke-on-Trent, Trentham

DePalma, R and Atkinson, E (2009) 'Permission to talk about it': narratives of sexualities equality in the primary classroom. *Qualitative Inquiry* 15(7) 876-892

DePalma, R and Atkinson, E (2009) Beyond tolerance: challenging heteronormativity in primary schools through reflective action research. *British Educational Research Journal,* 35(6) 837-855

DePalma, R and Jennett, M (2007) Deconstructing heteronormativity in primary schools in England: cultural approaches to a cultural phenomenon. In van Dijk, I and van Driel, B (eds) *Confronting Homophobia in Educational Practice* (19-32) Stoke-on-Trent, Trentham, 19-32

DePalma, R and Teague, L (2008) A democratic community of practice: unpicking all those words. *Educational Action Research* 16(4) 441-456

No Outsiders project team (2008) Using children's literature to challenge homophobia in primary schools. In DePalma, R and Atkinson, E (eds) *Invisible Boundaries: Addressing Sexualities Equality in Children's Worlds* (139-144). Stoke-on-Trent: Trentham, 139-144

Youdell, D (in press) *School Trouble: identity, power and politics in education*. London, Routledge

Also available from Trentham

INVISIBLE BOUNDARIES

addressing sexualities equality in children's worlds

Edited by Renée DePalma and Elizabeth Atkinson

This book tells the stories of children's experiences of lesbian, gay, bisexual and transgender identities in their families, communities, personal lives and schools.

Researchers, practitioners, interest groups, policy makers and young people came together over 18 months until May 2007 in an exciting and innovative project. The narrative and analysis that emerged opens a new arena for everyone working with children. It presents

- new ways of conceptualising and overcoming homophobia and transphobia in educational settings
- ideas about how to translate policy supporting sexualities equality into the experiences of children and their families
- the voices of young LGBT people speaking about their experiences of childhood
- fresh insights for people who work with children and have not considered the importance of sexualities equality for children's lives
- a vital contribution to building a fairer society

Contributors include Mark Jennett, author of *Stand up for us*, the British government guidelines on challenging homophobia in schools; Stephen Whittle, trans activist and professor of equalities law; members of Lesbian and Gay Youth Manchester; members of the *No Outsiders* research team challenging homophobia in primary schools; Sue Sanders, co-chair of Schools Out and teacher David Watkins.

This is an important book for anyone living or working with children: parents, teachers, community workers, voluntary workers, and all those brought under the broad scope of children's services across the UK, and equivalent services elsewhere. It brings together the voices of people from many sectors who realise the urgency of addressing issues of sexualities equality early on in children's lives.

ISBN 978 1 85856 430 2, 172 pages, 234 x 154mm, £19.99

www.trentham-books.co.uk

INTERROGATING HETERONORMATIVITY IN PRIMARY SCHOOLS

The *No Outsiders* Project

Edited by Renée DePalma and Elizabeth Atkinson

Primary teachers and other professionals working with children are increasingly required to address equality in relation to sexual orientation and gender expression as legislation in the UK and elsewhere includes lesbian, gay, bisexual and transgender rights in the equalities spectrum.

The *No Outsiders* Project has taken groundbreaking steps in addressing lesbian, gay, bisexual and transgender equality in primary schools. The *No Outsiders* Project is a collaboration of primary education practitioners and university researchers, funded by the ESRC. In this book, members of the research team analyse the issues which have permeated the team's challenge to heteronormativity and gender conformity in and through primary education and there is a chapter by Susan Talburt.

Together they explore the key themes of the project's work:

- silence and speaking out
- faith and culture
- leadership and role-modelling
- personal and emotional investment
- gay rights/liberal humanist and queer perspectives
- safety and risk-taking
- the possibility of a queer pedagogy
- intersections between queer theory and practice.

This is the academic companion to the team's practice-focused book which draws on the project teachers' classroom work, *Undoing Homophobia in Primary Schools* and follows their insightful *Invisible Boundaries: addressing sexualities equality in children's worlds*. It will be essential reading for all those in primary education who are concerned to challenge this last bastion of inequality, as well as for students and researchers in sociology, cultural studies, queer studies and related fields where the underlying discourses shaping heteronormativity and gender conformity require urgent analysis in the move towards a fairer society.

ISBN 978 1 85856 458 6, 186 pages, 234 x 156mm, £19.99